The Rules of Logic

Letter from the General Editor

The Library of Arabic Literature makes available Arabic editions and English translations of significant works of Arabic literature, with an emphasis on the seventh to nineteenth centuries. The Library of Arabic Literature thus includes texts from the pre-Islamic era to the cusp of the modern period, and encompasses a wide range of genres, including poetry, poetics, fiction, religion, philosophy, law, science, travel writing, history, and historiography.

Books in the series are edited and translated by internationally recognized scholars. They are published as hardcovers in parallel-text format with Arabic and English on facing pages, as English-only paperbacks, and as downloadable Arabic editions. For some texts, the series also publishes separate scholarly editions with full critical apparatus.

The Library encourages scholars to produce authoritative Arabic editions, accompanied by modern, lucid English translations, with the ultimate goal of introducing Arabic's rich literary heritage to a general audience of readers as well as to scholars and students.

The publications of the Library of Arabic Literature are generously supported by Tamkeen under the NYU Abu Dhabi Research Institute Award G1003 and are published by NYU Press.

Philip F. Kennedy
General Editor, Library of Arabic Literature

الرسالة الشمسيّة في القواعد المنطقيّة

نجم الدين الكاتبيّ

LIBRARY OF
المكتبة
ARABIC
العربية
LITERATURE

The Rules of Logic

Najm al-Dīn al-Kātibī

Edited and translated by
Tony Street

Volume editor
Joseph E. Lowry

NEW YORK UNIVERSITY PRESS
New York

NEW YORK UNIVERSITY PRESS
New York

Library of Congress Cataloging-in-Publication Control Number: 2023024967

Please contact the Library of Congress for Cataloging-in-Publication data.

ISBN: 9781479880249 (hardback)
ISBN: 9781479864706 (library ebook)
ISBN: 9781479819546 (consumer ebook)

New York University Press books are printed on acid-free paper,
and their binding materials are chosen for strength and durability.

Series design by Titus Nemeth.

Typeset in Tasmeem, using DecoType Naskh and Emiri.

Typesetting and digitization by Stuart Brown.

Manufactured in the United States of America
c10 9 8 7 6 5 4 3 2 1

Table of Contents

Acknowledgments

Warm thanks to James Montgomery for entrusting *al-Risālah al-Shamsiyyah* to me in the first place, and for keeping faith over the years as I allowed myself to be distracted by other things. Joe Lowry has been an ideal editor; he has saved me from countless mistakes, alerted me to glaring omissions, and rallied my spirits when they flagged. LAL's editorial director Dr Chip Rossetti has been supportive throughout, and LAL's digital production manager Stuart Brown went beyond the call of duty and made substantive improvements to the content.

Many other people have helped, often without knowing, and most in more ways than I can record. Thanks to Nicholas Rescher for having paved everyone's path to the study of Arabic logic, to Tony Johns for introducing me to Fakhr al-Dīn al-Rāzī, to Father Georges Anawati for confirming me as a follower of al-Rāzī, and to Richard Frank for insisting I look beyond al-Rāzī. A timely phone call from Dimitri Gutas was the only thing that kept me in Islamic studies. Paul Thom has generously helped over the years as I struggled with the material. Asad Ahmed, Ahmed Alwishah, Feriel Bouhafa, Reza Dadkhah, Silvia Di Vincenzo, Asad Fallahi, Pree Jareonsettasin, Jari Kaukua, Dustin Klinger, Harun Kuşlu, Joep Lameer, Stephen Menn, Yoav Meyrav, Reza Pourjavady, Boaz Schuman, Ayman Shihadeh, Rob Wisnovsky, Walter Young, and Behnam Zolghadr have helped me obtain manuscripts or solve interpretive problems. Colleagues close by—John Marenbon, Catherine Pickstock, and Yasser Qureshy—have made medieval philosophy at Cambridge deeply congenial. Colleagues farther afield have had the kindness to involve me in projects from which I have learned things crucial to understanding *al-Risālah al-Shamsiyyah*: Peter Adamson, Leone Gazziero, Nadja Germann, Yehuda Halper, Charles Manekin, and Shahid Rahman. I have learned more from my (mostly former) students than they have from me: Suf Amichay, Amal Awad, Necmeddin Besikci, Zhenyu Cai, Daniel Davies, Tareq Moqbel, Mohammed Saleh Zarepour, and Tianyi Zhang.

I owe special thanks to three former colleagues at Cambridge. Khaled El-Rouayheb came more than twenty years ago; his extraordinary work since then has transformed the study of Arabic logic. He has always been generous to a fault in sharing manuscripts and insights. At roughly the same time, Cornelia Schöck also arrived; she made me aware of the huge importance of the connections between logic and the broader Islamic sciences. After leaving for Bochum, Cornelia was awarded a grant from the DFG (German Research Foundation) that employed Riccardo Strobino, and in an act of monumental kindness allowed him to base himself in Cambridge. Riccardo's time here was certainly the happiest period of my academic career. If my translation has any fidelity to the original, or clarity in expression, it is entirely due to watching Riccardo go about his work.

Above all, much love and many thanks to Ruth for putting up with it all.

Introduction

Logic was revered in the thirteenth century, perhaps more highly than it has been revered before or since. This is as true of the Muslim East as it is of the Christian West. It has recently been said of Peter of Spain's *Summaries of Logic*, probably written in the 1230s, that no other book on logic prior to the twentieth century had such wide readership or, in consequence, did so much to shape Western ways of constructing well-formed sentences and putting them together in valid arguments.[1] But perhaps one other logic text has had just as many readers, and as profound an impact on ways of formal discourse and argument. In the Muslim East, *al-Risālah al-Shamsiyyah* (literally *The Epistle [on Logical Rules] for Shams al-Dīn*, but which I am publishing under the title *The Rules of Logic*) was written some forty years after the *Summaries*, by someone who was Peter's exact contemporary: Najm al-Dīn al-Kātibī (d. 675/1276). *The Rules of Logic* also came to figure in the education of nearly every aspiring young scholar, and is still read in traditional schools.

Logic in the Muslim East

How did logic come to be so important in the syllabus of Muslim schools? From the moment the armies first came out of the Arabian Peninsula, Muslims found themselves in control of communities that had studied logic for centuries, and that—in the case of the Syriac Christians—had made it a central feature of religious education. But it is not until late in the Umayyad period (ca. 44–132/661–750) that we have clear evidence of Muslim interest in logic, specifically among courtiers of the regime, one of whom translated an introductory text based on Porphyry's *Introduction*, and Aristotle's *Categories*, *De Interpretatione*, and the first seven chapters of the *Prior Analytics*.[2] This interest intensified dramatically with the Abbasids (ca. 132–656/750–1258), when the needs of propaganda—the need to be seen to adopt Sasanian cultural projects—led the dynasty to support networks of translators of scientific literature drawn from the various religious communities. From the early ninth century, Baghdad was home to a number of translation projects, increasingly devoted to producing full translations of the texts that make up the Aristotelian *Organon.* The culmination of the work of these translators was the emergence of a textual Aristotelianism in the first quarter of the tenth century, led by the Muslim Abū Naṣr al-Fārābī (d. 339/950) and the Christian Abū Bishr Mattā ibn Yūnus (d. 328/940). Much of their output can be seen as a continuation of the late antique commentators, producing careful and often critical analyses of the Aristotelian texts on logic.

The commentary work continued through the first half of the eleventh century in Baghdad's school of loosely affiliated scholars, only to be rudely interrupted by a letter from a rising young star, Avicenna (Ibn Sīnā; d. 428/1037), who was working at the time in Hamadhān, asking the Baghdadi scholars details about their doctrine on universals.[3] Here was a philosopher who, seemingly outside of any scholarly network, had come to his own quite radical take on Aristotelian logic, who could defend his views with crushingly cogent arguments, and who—at the time of the letter to the Baghdadis—was in the process of presenting his views in various genres designed to appeal to different audiences, and to students at different stages in their education. Early on there was resistance to Avicenna's logic,[4] but fairly rapidly it became the standard system against which an Arabic logician would define his own position. The Aristotelian *Organon* was effectively replaced by the Avicennian logical corpus; indeed, reference to the First Teacher (Aristotle) dwindled, only to be replaced by constant reference to Avicenna, the Leading Master (*al-shaykh al-ra'īs*).

Throughout this period, from the early third/ninth to the late fifth/eleventh century, logic was still confined to networks of scholars associated more with courts, or institutions like hospitals and observatories, than with any given religion. At the same time, there was some anxiety among pious believers—whether Muslims, Jews, or Christians—that by studying the methods by which Aristotle arrived at his heretical beliefs, the student could end up holding the same beliefs. Lawyers and theologians learned no logic in their studies, or at any rate, no logic derived from the Aristotelian *Organon.* Against this trend, al-Fārābī wrote a work in the early fourth/tenth century designed to show that Aristotelian logic could contribute to legal studies a deeper understanding of forensic argument techniques. It is difficult to assign a single reason behind the ultimate acceptance of logic in Muslim institutions of learning, but there can be no doubt that the utility of logic for analyzing and justifying legal reasoning was a major consideration. Among others, the renowned scholar Abū Ḥāmid al-Ghazālī (d. 505/1111) took up this line of defense, and even prefaced his summa of jurisprudence, the *Distillation of the Principles of Jurisprudence* (*al-Mustaṣfā min ʿilm al-uṣūl*), with an introduction on logic.[5]

Al-Kātibī's Life, Logic, Works, and Significance

Due to Avicenna's victory over conservative Aristotelianism, al-Kātibī's *The Rules of Logic* presents a logic strongly marked by Avicenna, and divergent in many ways from the logic in Peter's *Summaries*. Due to widespread acceptance of the claim that logic was helpful for legal studies, *The Rules of Logic*'s major reception was not among scholars working in courts and scientific institutions, but in the religious schools, among Muslim students of law and theology. It is ironic that a work commended so highly by the *fatāwā*, the legal opinions, was written by someone working in an observatory funded by monies usurped from religious trusts, but so it was: al-Kātibī was one of the founding members of the Īl-Khānid observatory at Marāghah, on which work began in 657/1259.[6] The Shams al-Dīn to whom al-Kātibī dedicated his *Rules* was the regime's vizier, who had come to power in 661/1263. This means that the *Rules*'s dedication, and probably its composition, postdate 1263.

Najm al-Dīn Abū l-Ḥasan ʿAlī ibn ʿUmar al-Kātibī was born in 600/1204 in Qazvīn, about a hundred miles west of modern Tehran. A member of the Shāfiʿī school of law, the "al-Kātibī" in his name may mean he had connections of some kind with the scribal class. He went off to study the rational sciences with Athīr al-Dīn al-Abharī (d. ca. 660/1261), and manuscripts from that period of study survive to this day in al-Kātibī's hand.[7] The most important political event that unfolded through al-Kātibī's lifetime was the Mongol invasion and the sack of Baghdad (656/1258), among other cities. Catastrophic as the event was for many, for al-Kātibī it seems mainly to have presented him with a golden opportunity. In the late 1250s, he was approached by the famous Shiʿi scholar Naṣīr al-Dīn al-Ṭūsī (d. 672/1274), and enlisted to help found the Īl-Khānid observatory at Marāghah, far to the west of Qazvīn. Al-Kātibī taught a number of students, among them the famous Shiʿi theologian al-ʿAllāmah al-Ḥillī (d. 726/1325); there were others, but al-Ḥillī was the one who mattered most for the reception of the *Rules*. Al-Kātibī seems by and large to have remained teaching in Marāghah until shortly before his death, and probably died there in 675/1276; he was buried in Qazvīn.[8]

The fact that al-Kātibī studied with al-Abharī is extremely significant, because al-Abharī is said to have been a student of Fakhr al-Dīn al-Rāzī (d. 606/1210; more likely he was a student of one of al-Rāzī's students),[9] and al-Rāzī is one of the three most important intellectual coordinates for al-Kātibī's work, along with Avicenna and Afḍal al-Dīn al-Khūnajī (d. 646/1248). Indeed, al-Kātibī is described as one of the followers of Fakhr al-Dīn (*min atbāʿ Fakhr al-Dīn*) by al-Ḥillī, so al-Abharī must have managed to convey to al-Kātibī a vivid sense of al-Rāzī's intellectual project. In broad terms, al-Rāzī's project was to recruit the philosophy of Avicenna for the service of Islamic theology, making the logic the core of theological methods of argument. This involved commentary on one of Avicenna's major works, *Pointers and Reminders* (*Kitāb al-Ishārāt wa-l-tanbīhāt*), and criticism of many of the principles it invokes; it also involved the composition of independent works in which traditional theological topics were developed with heavy use of philosophical concepts.

Just as al-Rāzī mediated al-Kātibī's reception of Avicenna, al-Khūnajī mediated his reception of al-Rāzī, mainly of the logic. Al-Khūnajī had ceaselessly and critically evaluated al-Rāzī's logical work, and pushed it in an ever more formal direction. So, while al-Rāzī had set *Pointers and Reminders* as the focus for much later work on Avicenna's logic, and established a number of crucial research questions and distinctions with which to deal with these questions, al-Khūnajī critically evaluated both al-Rāzī's distinctions and his arguments. Al-Kātibī often took up al-Khūnajī's refinements and alternative arguments, but often also defended al-Rāzī or introduced further refinements. However well al-Kātibī got on with his colleague al-Ṭūsī at the observatory, over logic they must have argued endlessly: al-Ṭūsī would never have been prepared to treat al-Rāzī and al-Khūnajī as though their arguments were on par with Avicenna's.

Al-Kātibī is almost as famous for a work that covered metaphysics and physics, *Philosophy of the Source* (*Ḥikmat al-ʿayn*), as concise and beautifully structured as the *Rules*, and consequently equally popular in the schoolroom. He wrote a companion text on logic for the *Philosophy of the Source*, the *Source of the Precepts* (*ʿAyn al-qawāʿid*), and he wrote the long *Compendium of Subtleties in the Disclosure of Truths* (*Jāmiʿ al-daqāʾiq fī kashf al-ḥaqāʾiq*). He wrote other short treatises and epistles, and a commentary on al-Rāzī's text on philosophical theology, the *Treatise on the Thoughts of Ancient and Recent Scholars* (*Muḥaṣṣal afkār al-mutaqaddimīn wa-l-mutaʾakhkhirīn*). He also wrote two massive commentaries, on al-Rāzī's *Epitome of Logic and Philosophy* (*al-Mulakhkhaṣ fī l-manṭiq wa-l-ḥikmah*; I only consult the logic volume, published under the title

Manṭiq al-Mulakhkhaṣ) and al-Khūnajī's *Disclosure of Secrets from the Obscurities of Thought* (*Kashf al-asrār ʿan ghawāmiḍ al-afkār*). Al-Kātibī was, in short, first and foremost a philosopher with a special interest in logic.

The Rules of Logic is a text that was read by nearly every aspiring scholar in the central territories of the Islamic world, through what has been called the Late Middle Period, and—in traditional schools—it is still read today.[10] One measure of its extraordinary standing as a high-level introductory text for the study of logic is the number of manuscripts of it we find in libraries that hold Arabic collections. Likewise, when lithography and printing became common in the Muslim world, numerous versions of the *Rules* were made available. Most of these manuscripts and printed versions give the text of the *Rules*, along with one of the many commentaries written on it, especially the commentary of Quṭb al-Dīn al-Rāzī al-Taḥtānī (d. 766/1365). Even the British East India Company joined in, producing what is probably the first movable-type version of the text, along with al-Taḥtānī's commentary. Indeed, another way to gauge the scale of the *Rules*'s impact is in terms of these commentaries; it is certainly among the texts most commented upon in Muslim scholarly circles. The focus of the commentators changed over time, and this was a factor in the *Rules*'s continued recognition as a central teaching text. Commentaries would dwell on subjects touched on in the text, contingent on the central focus in approaching the discipline as that focus changed through the centuries and across regions. And, of course, the commentaries continued to be written because the *Rules* had found a secure place in the syllabus of many religious colleges. For whatever reason, even those scholars who regarded the broader logical tradition with suspicion were prepared to include the *Rules* among texts unobjectionable to pious concerns.[11]

Reception of the *Rules*

A text lives in readers' reception of it; the way readers through the ages have received *The Rules of Logic* is set out for us in the many commentaries written on it. Before I say a few words about the commentators I have used to understand the *Rules* and assess its reception, let me say something about the place Aristotle and Avicenna have among the authorities invoked by the *Rules*.

Most notable by his absence is Aristotle. Al-Kātibī makes no reference to Aristotle, though admittedly he makes no direct reference to anyone at all. But if we fill out the authorities al-Kātibī is tacitly invoking by looking at what his commentators say (and in particular al-Ḥillī, who studied the text under his guidance), the point remains: neither Aristotle nor his work occupies al-Kātibī's attention. Before I turn to Avicenna, who does have that honor, I should note that this does not mean that Arabic logicians did not recognize Aristotle's ultimate primacy in the discipline. Al-Rāzī could think of no higher compliment to pay al-Shāfiʿī than that he was to jurisprudence what Aristotle was to logic.[12] The respected bibliographer Ibn al-Akfānī (d. 749/1348) says much the same (along with some questionable chronology):

> It is widely known that the person who originated and instituted logic is Aristotle, that he found no other book [on logic] by his predecessors other than a book on the categories, and that he was alerted to writing logic down and putting it in that order by the organization of Euclid's book on geometry.[13]

But respect did not mean a student should devote time to reading the translations of Aristotle's logic that were available. Ibn al-Akfānī went on to set out a syllabus for the student of logic, and it is noteworthy that even someone who is prepared to read "the vast ocean of the logic part" of Avicenna's *Cure* (*Kitāb al-Shifāʾ*) is not advised to read Aristotle's logical works. Even so, there was a continuing sense that it was valid to evaluate at least some aspects of what the Arabic logicians were doing in terms of what Aristotle had done. This is what the great intellectual historian Ibn Khaldūn (d. 784/1382) did (following al-Taftāzānī) in a much-quoted passage in which he criticizes post-Avicennian logic for failing to cover the valuable uses of logic set out in the books, the *Posterior Analytics*, the *Topics*, the *Rhetoric*, the *Poetics*, and the *Sophistical Refutations*.[14] But—to return to the primary point—we do not find the textual engagement with Aristotle that shapes so much Latin philosophy, nor any appeal to his authority on substantive matters.

It is Avicenna who towers over al-Kātibī's *The Rules of Logic*, who replaces Aristotle in every sense, whose presence is underlined at every turn by the commentators. But Avicenna is for al-Kātibī as old as Kant is for us, and the logicians mentioned earlier—al-Rāzī and al-Khūnajī—played a huge role in how al-Kātibī read Avicenna. Indeed, Ibn al-Akfānī recommends that the aspiring logician read al-Kātibī's commentaries on the logic texts of both of his great post-Avicennian mentors.[15] But rather than go back to the books that make up al-Kātibī's canon of authorities to try to work out how he is responding to his predecessors, I have turned to three of the earliest commentators on the *Rules*: al-ʿAllāmah al-Ḥillī, Quṭb al-Dīn al-Rāzī al-Taḥtānī, and Saʿd al-Dīn al-Taftāzānī (d. 792/1390). They have clarified many points for the translation.

A few words on these early commentators is necessary to cast some light on the process of the *Rules*'s early reception. Al-Ḥillī is a young man writing one of his earliest books when composing *Clear Precepts in Commentary on the Epistle for Shams al-Dīn* (*al-Qawāʿid al-jaliyyah fī sharḥ al-Risālah al-Shamsiyyah*); he intends to provide (so we are told) guidance for his young colleagues trying to read a difficult text. (I would note that, at first glance, *The Rules of Logic* does not look so difficult, so al-Ḥillī's colleagues are at least advanced enough to resist being lulled into a false sense of security by the *Rules*'s brisk and straightforward tone.) Al-Ḥillī's major point of difference from al-Taḥtānī and al-Taftāzānī is that he writes a second, deeper book in tandem with the *Clear Precepts*, *Hidden Secrets* (*al-Asrār al-khafiyyah fī l-ʿulūm al-ʿaqliyyah*), and thus feels able for the most part to leave disputed points up in the air. These are especially the points at which al-Kātibī departs from Avicenna and follows al-Rāzī.

Al-Taḥtānī is a more senior scholar than al-Ḥillī was when he writes his commentary, *Redaction of the Rules of Logic in Commentary on the Epistle for Shams al-Dīn* (*Taḥrīr al-qawāʿid al-manṭiqiyyah fī sharḥ al-Risālah al-Shamsiyyah*), and he settles to each point (especially early in the commentary) with thorough and slightly self-satisfied precision. The sense I have is that he is more aligned with al-Kātibī's views on the subject, and even though he corrects a number of claims in the *Rules*, he rarely displays hostility toward al-Kātibī's broader program, or the authorities on which he draws for inspiration.

Al-Taftāzānī is engaged in a second-order commentary, *Commentary on the Epistle for Shams al-Dīn* (*Sharḥ al-Risālah al-Shamsiyyah*), correcting al-Taḥtānī. He has a reputation—probably undeserved—for plodding scholarship,[16] and writes his commentary to clarify and at points deepen al-Taḥtānī's *Redaction*. Al-Taftāzānī was drawn into a debilitating enmity with a younger scholar, al-Sayyid al-Sharīf al-Jurjānī (d. 816/1413), who wrote marginal notes (a *ḥāshiyah*) on the *Redaction*; the work by al-Jurjānī is much shorter than al-Taftāzānī's, and is printed in the margins or footnotes of many versions of the *Redaction* (including the edition I use, by Bīdārfar).

My sense is that al-Ḥillī's commentary is the clearest of the three, but it is also the most hostile, and its charity grows thinner the more al-Kātibī diverges from Avicenna.[17] Further, although each commentary has its virtues, none covers every point that seems important to me. So al-Taḥtānī alone presents tables of the modal mixes (sadly garbled in the Bīdārfar printing); at the same time, he often fails to give details for the scholars on whom al-Kātibī draws, or from whom he distances himself. For example, although al-Taḥtānī gives the different truth-conditions for the coincidental conditional set out in §60, he fails to note which Avicenna prefers, though al-Ḥillī does. Similarly, al-Ḥillī draws attention to—and deplores—the fact that al-Kātibī is following al-Rāzī in his taxonomy of definitions in §36, whereas al-Taḥtānī simply delivers al-Kātibī's account without complaint. Al-Taftāzānī's commentary stands as an independent work much more than we would expect given its declared intention—dealing with what al-Taḥtānī had neglected, resolving problems arising from his zeal for explanation, pinning down his loose phrasing—but nonetheless he assumes more advanced knowledge of the subject on the part of his readers than either of his predecessors.

In reading *The Rules of Logic* under the spell of the great early commentaries, I encountered a number of surprises. On many occasions, I have read a lemma of the *Rules* and thought it straightforward, only to discover from the commentators a tangle of difficulties I simply had not seen. Take, for the earliest example of this, the first lemma; the subtlety of the resolutions and refinements of the phrasing (how does al-Kātibī intend us to take the disjunctive?) and of the material being treated (if a conception is actually a component of an assertion, rather than merely a precondition for it, how can the two be opposed?) is difficult to convey. I have also been surprised by the questions, both those addressed and those that are not raised, not just in the reception of the *Rules*, but in its initial composition. Why dwell so long, for example, on the aspects of signification theory set out in §§7–14 (and especially those set out in the first three lemmata), and not—given that the *Rules* is meant for students early in their logical studies—say something about how to define signification, and to distinguish in particular conventional signification?

At the end of reading the *Rules*, one may wonder what students of the text would have gained from their efforts. Theories of signification and predication, obviously, along with analyses of quantified, modalized, and hypothetical propositions; procedures for checking inferences; and the outlines of a philosophy of science. But, in the most general terms, they would have come to realize with what indeterminate materials natural language operates—the shifting significations of expressions, the overtones of meanings, and the deep ambiguities hidden in seemingly clear sentences—and the lengths to which one must go to make these aspects of language determinate. I suspect that few of the *Rules*'s readers went on to formulate knowledge-claims in the propositional forms listed in the *Rules,* and still fewer went on to deduce new knowledge-claims using the inference-schemata al-Kātibī had proved to be valid. But all would have come away from their study with an appreciation of the many pitfalls of building an argument or setting out an unambiguous claim in a natural language.

They were also made aware of a culturally revered canon of philosophical authority, one that freed their own culture from adherence to strictly Aristotelian forms. Reading the commentaries showed that no reference needed to be made beyond Arabic texts, and "the ancients" (*al-qudamā'*) only rarely recall a logician more ancient than al-Fārābī. Learning how all important problems were generated and resolved within the *Rules*'s canon drove home more memorably than anything else could the resources of Arabic philosophical culture. We need not wonder how logic fitted so snugly into a legal and theological education: it reasserted rather than unsettled the independence of Arabic scholarship.

Note on the Text

The Arabic Text

By and large, I follow the text of *The Rules of Logic* given as lemmata in Tabrīziyān's edition of al-Ḥillī's *Clear Rules* (T, or ت in the footnotes; it omits the dedication, my §0, which I take from Ṣāliḥ's edition of al-Taftāzānī's *Commentary*). There are many manuscripts of the *Rules*, and—generally with one or other of its early commentaries—many printings and editions, some more critical than others. I have consulted three manuscripts. The earliest, al-Astānah al-Raḍawiyyah 1114 (R, ر) dates to 679/1280-81, three years after al-Kātibī's death, and includes the commentary by al-Ḥillī.[18] The second oldest (S, س) is given in the *Ark of Tabrīz* (*Safīna-yi Tabrīz*), a codex with a number of texts precious to Abū l-Majd Muḥammad ibn Masʿūd al-Tabrīzī, a scribe famous in his day, and copied between 721/1321 and 723/1323 (now available in facsimile).[19] This is a beautiful manuscript in a minute hand, but notably has no corrections. The third manuscript, Trinity R.13.54 (K, ك), is noted in Palmer's catalogue of Arabic manuscripts at Trinity College in Cambridge, where it is claimed that it is a holograph.[20]

The oldest witness, R, is extremely valuable; it is, however, primarily a witness to al-Ḥillī's commentary, and omits the opening material of the *Rules*. The rare occasions I would question it is when S offers a different reading in a stretch of text that suffers no other obvious problem. I apply such a convoluted test because of the extraordinary nature of the *Ark*. Late though it is (at least, relative to R), the text in the *Ark* is presented free of commentary, by a renowned scribe who had access to the finest manuscripts available in his day. What matters, however, is that the scribe of the *Ark*, at least when he was copying the *Rules*, was determined to produce a minutely rendered text that looked flawless. There is no marginal correction, no overwriting, no interlinear activity; when an error was made, on he wrote, without a backward glance. The scribe of the *Rules* in the *Ark* aspires to a page without blemish of emendation. When it makes sense, I have given great weight to the text in the *Ark*, but when it has obvious gaps, I have attributed this to scribal vanity. Would that K were, as its colophon claims, a holograph. Even though Adam Gacek has dashed that hope,[21] it remains a relatively early manuscript of the text alone, with marginal and interlinear corrections; it is in agreement more often than not with the other two manuscripts. I use it mainly as a preponderating consideration, and only a few times as a lone voice of correction.

The outcome of examining these three witnesses of the *Rules* in this way has led me to adopt Tabrīziyān's edition for nearly all the Arabic text that follows. To consider alternative readings left to one side by his edition, I have consulted three among the many printed versions of the *Rules*: the edition by Aloys Sprenger and his team, that by M. Faḍlallāh (F, ف), and the recent version of al-Taḥtānī's *Redaction* by M. Bīdārfar, which gives the *Rules* in its lemmata.[22] The last two embrace roughly the same approach to establishing the text. Faḍlallāh seeks to use a number of earlier printings to establish an integrated version aiming at grammatical correctness and orthographic consistency; on two occasions in the text that follows, I adopt his reading.[23] Bīdārfar's text is derived from two Cairo printings.[24] There is no account of how Sprenger's text was established, but it observes grammatical agreement and provides all vowels. Somewhat arbitrarily, I have taken Faḍlallāh's variants as representative of the range of material left out of Tabrīziyān's text. The variants involve decisions that are, from my point of view, fairly harmless. Most often, they involve phrases designed to fill out al-Kātibī's lean exposition. Of even less consequence, some variants give different examples to make the same point, or different but synonymous expressions. Points of crucial difference are, I think, rare. I expose myself as someone who should leave the editing of texts to others when I say this: if the primary goal is to set before the reader the text students have read through the centuries, we need to recognize that the *Rules* has been so long embedded in commentary that trying to cut it back to what al-Kātibī actually wrote can look like quixotic nostalgia.

The text is given with minimal punctuation and minimal voweling. I have left the numbers as they are in Tabrīziyān's edition, even when one of the manuscripts gives them closer to classical rules of agreement. I have departed from Middle Arabic orthographic conventions for the hamzah.

The text is divided into short lemmata numbered so that they by and large correspond to the division into passages for comment that is given in most printings of the *Rules* with al-Taḥtānī's commentary.[25] Sadly, this differs from the division given by al-Ḥillī (my favorite among the commentators), but al-Taḥtānī has an unassailable status in the tradition of reading the *Rules*. I hope that many who read the *Rules* will want to go on to read a commentary on it, and the lemmata numbered as in printings of al-Taḥtānī's commentary should facilitate that second reading. Within the passages al-Taḥtānī identifies, I sometimes introduce even finer subdivisions, highlighting what seem to me to be separate topics (§52 is a case in point, especially when compared with §53 and following).

Whereas the various divisions into passages for comment are posthumous, the tight structure of the text itself, reflected in the sectioning of my translation, is all al-Kātibī's work; I have merely given as headings and subheadings parts of the text of the *Rules*. The minute script of manuscript S means that the *Rules* can be fitted onto five sides of folio, and the structure is available to a sweep of the eye: a discipline unfolding under rubrications as al-Kātibī divided it. It is, in a real sense, a universal table of contents, one that does service for countless post-Mongol logic texts in Arabic.

The English Translation

The Rules of Logic was edited and translated into English by Aloys Sprenger and William Kay in the 1850s. Their translation is an extremely helpful point of reference, which guided me in my early encounter with the *Rules*, and against which I have checked my work at the end. Sprenger left the section on the modal syllogistic out of the translation (§§98–104 in the following text), and provided few notes on the *Rules* to help the reader. It was more than a hundred years later that Nicholas Rescher came back to translate the omitted section.[26] Even before I read Sprenger-Kay, I had read Rescher's introductions and analyses of al-Kātibī's logic, and the translation is guided by an interpretation of the syllogistic that owes its main lines to Rescher.[27] I have also followed Rescher in adopting Sprenger's translations of the names of the various modal propositions for my version of the *Rules*; this decision has a few curious consequences (for example, the English "conditional" applies both to one kind of categorical proposition and to one kind of hypothetical), but will hopefully make it slightly easier to refer back to earlier work on the *Rules*.

Given its debts to earlier work, it is fair to ask whether the translation offered here represents the original text more clearly or more faithfully than its predecessor. I hope it does; and if it does, it will be for two reasons. One lies in the field's increasing grip on Avicennian and post-Avicennian philosophy, and the increasing availability of texts from the community in which al-Kātibī worked. In particular, recent editions of the works of al-Rāzī and al-Khūnajī allow us to see al-Kātibī's work as the outcome of a century-long project of assimilating Avicennian logic. The other reason is that, as noted above, I have decided to follow in the footsteps of al-Kātibī's main early commentators, al-Ḥillī, al-Taḥtānī, and al-Taftāzānī. I concede that they may be wrong on points in interpreting the *Rules*, but they (especially al-Ḥillī) are closely acquainted with al-Kātibī's central concerns, and strive to order the text according to these concerns. For the future, the most important single resource for guiding a fresh translation of al-Kātibī will be al-Kātibī's other logical works, nearly all of which remain in manuscript as of the time of writing this introduction.[28]

There is a grand tradition of translating medieval Latin logic into English—one need only think of Brian P. Copenhaver and his team, of Paul Thom, and above all of Gyula Klima—and the resulting translations are readable in ways that reflect a consensus on how to approach the task.[29] There are certainly accurate translations of Arabic logic texts—F. W. Zimmermann's translation of al-Fārābī's commentary on *De Interpretatione* still deserves honorable mention, even though his work has now been joined by a number of other worthy efforts (see Further Reading)—but the results have yet to converge on an agreed way to translate the terms of art. More than any other work to which I refer, Riccardo Strobino's entry on Avicenna's logic in the Stanford Encyclopedia of Philosophy serves as a glossary for the vast majority of the terms translated in the text that follows;[30] I hope this makes the task of putting al-Kātibī's logic in the context of the most important authority from which it derives somewhat easier. I also believe Strobino's entry reflects an emerging consensus on how to translate the terms.

This is a translation of a text written within a group of scholars whose activities grew out of translations made long ago, but who, as a group, avoided working with translated texts, which they believed must be misleading. They were right. I have hesitated when choosing among possible translations for technical terms, and I refer here to a few of those hesitations, chosen to illustrate some of the considerations at play. The first is perhaps the most difficult to resolve. Like other premodern logicians, al-Kātibī presented his logic in a natural language or, more precisely, did not present his logic by translating arguments into a formal language. At the same time, the sentence forms into which he regiments his propositions for logical treatment are hardly idiomatic Arabic; aside from anything else, they can involve opaque hangovers from the translation movement. Take as an example the absolute proposition (*al-qaḍiyyah al-muṭlaqah*) as set out in §78;

the Arabic for the a-proposition would read *bi-l-iṭlāq al-ʿāmm kull jīm bāʾ*. One way to render this is in parallel with the structurally similar necessity proposition (*al-qaḍiyyah al-ḍarūriyyah*), for which *bi-l-ḍarūrah kull jīm bāʾ* is clearly "by necessity, every C is B." With Strobino, I render *bi-l-iṭlāq al-ʿāmm* with the clumsy phrase "general absoluteness," but the origin of the Arabic is cloudy, and its earliest usage is at variance with al-Kātibī's.[31] We are told that the contradictory of "by general absoluteness, every C is B" (*bi-l-iṭlāq al-ʿāmm kull jīm bāʾ*) is "always, some C is not B" (*dāʾiman baʿḍ jīm laysa bāʾ*; §69.2), so, however it is expressed, the general absolute should be understood as "every C is at least once B." Given that no native speaker innocent of Avicenna's logic would take this understanding from *bi-l-iṭlāq al-ʿāmm kull jīm bāʾ*, the translator has to decide whether the English should make the reader face the same difficulty as a pre-philosophical reader of the Arabic, or over-translate. I have chosen the first path for the translation. I hope the awkward phrasing in the translation reflects what I take to be al-Kātibī's intention: to make the language of regimentation awkward enough to signal that those passages should be read in a different register.

The second problem is often noted by translators in the Library of Arabic Literature series: there are words that are productive in Arabic for which no equally productive English term can be found. Take the example of *ʿāmm*, "general." The general absolute (*al-muṭlaqah al-ʿāmmah*) such as "every C is at least once B" is combined to make a second, two-sided absolute (§56 below, the non-perpetual existential): "every C is at least once B and at least once not B," referred to by al-Kātibī's commentators (but not by al-Kātibī himself, at least in the *Rules*) as the special absolute (*al-muṭlaqah al-khāṣṣah*). The general proposition (*ʿāmmah*) is implicationally weaker ("more general," *aʿamm*) than the special (*khāṣṣah*), in the sense that a two-sided absolute implies a one-sided one, but not the other way round. *ʿUmūm*, "generality," may also refer to the relative extension of terms; if between the two there is *ʿumūm muṭlaq* (§26 and following), the individuals under the more particular term are included in or form a subset of the individuals under the more general. Inconsistently, I translate "proper inclusion," not "absolute generality." In short, technical English obscures deeper links among the terms of art that are clear to the Arabic logicians.

Let me conclude with a couple of more minor worries. Ideally, the translation of a term should reflect its Greek provenance. Strictly, *qaḍiyyah ḥamliyyah* should be "predicative proposition," not "categorical proposition," but then it would no longer correspond to the common English rendition of the original phrase in Aristotle's logic; this consideration is generally decisive. On the other hand, once a term is translated into Arabic, its further development may depend on whether the productivity of the Arabic term is exploited. Take *lāzim* (literally "inseparable") as we find it in the translation of Porphyry's *Introduction* (the classical text introducing the material given in the first treatise of the *Rules*); Barnes's translation gives its corresponding Greek as "concomitant," now the most common translation of *lāzim*. But once in Arabic, *lāzim* the active participle invokes its passive participle *malzūm* ("what is followed"); together, they are used in technical phrases like *lāzim al-lāzim lāzim al-malzūm* ("the implicate of the implicate is the implicate of the implicant"; not in the *Rules*, but often called on by commentators when explaining later sections of the text). The English terms "implicate" and "implicant" may sound ugly and jar with modern logical usage, but unlike "concomitant" and its cognates, both at least appear in modern dictionaries (for example, the Oxford English Dictionary) with meanings that make sense of such technical phrases.

I close with one last consideration. Avicenna is the culmination of the late antique tradition of commentary on Aristotle, and it makes the most sense to translate him with words evocative of the Greek tradition in which he intervenes. But writers of the second wave of Avicennian philosophy, from the twelfth century on, are at best mediated in their reading of Aristotle, and indifferent to textual problems in the ancient tradition. Their concern is rather to contest the reading of Avicenna, and increasingly they contest that reading in theological venues. In this respect, the activities of later readers of Avicenna's logic among adherents of the Shāfiʿī school of legal thought and the Ashʿarī school of theology, like al-Kātibī, strongly resemble the activities of their contemporaries in the Latin West; ideally, a translation should be designed to recall these contemporaries more than al-Kātibī's discarded Greek predecessors.

Notes to the Introduction

1 Copenhaver et al., *Peter of Spain: Summaries of Logic: Text, Translation, Introduction, and Notes*, ix. Most references I make to Peter's *Summaries* are through Buridan's commentary on them; see Klima, *John Buridan, Summulae de Dialectica: An Annotated Translation, with a Philosophical Introduction.* Peter was a contemporary of al-Kātibī, and Buridan, Peter's greatest commentator, was a contemporary of al-Kātibī's commentator al-Taḥtānī.

2 Some of the convolutions of the early transmission are recently traced in Hermans, "A Persian Origin of the Arabic Aristotle? The Debate on the Circumstantial Evidence of the Manteq Revisited."

3 See an account in broad terms in Michot, *Ibn Sīnā: Lettre au Vizir Abū Saʿd*, 10*–14*; reference to the edition used is given by Michot on p. 134.

4 The reaction of Avicenna's contemporaries in Shiraz to his logic is examined in Street, "Avicenna's Twenty Questions on Logic: Preliminary Notes for Further Work."

5 On al-Fārābī's project, see for example Sabra's notes in his review of Rescher's *Al-Fārābī's Short Commentary on Aristotle's Prior Analytics*, 242. For al-Ghazālī's contribution, see the short account of his detractor, Averroes, *Le Philosophe et la Loi*, 122–23.

6 The classic account of the founding of the observatory is Sayılı, *The Observatory in Islam and Its Place in the General History of the Observatory*, 205; the finances are noted in passing in al-Rahim, *The Creation of Philosophical Tradition: Biography and the Reception of Avicenna's Philosophy from the Eleventh to the Fourteenth Centuries A.D.*, 106.

7 For a reproduction, see Eichner, "The Post-Avicennian Philosophical Tradition and Islamic Orthodoxy: Philosophical and Theological Summae in Context," 536.

8 Al-Rahim, *The Creation of Philosophical Tradition*, 107; al-Rahim's account of al-Kātibī (106–117) is a full and critical treatment of his life and work. For an account focused on his work on logic, see El-Rouayheb, *The Development of Arabic Logic (1200–1800)*, 56–59; for a resolution of doubts about date and likely place of death, see El-Rouayheb, "Al-Kātibī al-Qazwīnī."

9 Barhebraeus, *Specimen Historiae Arabum, Sive, Gregorii Abul Farajii Malatiensis de Origine & Moribus Arabum Succincta Narratio*, 485.

10 I adopt the periodization of Islamic history in Hodgson; see his *The Venture of Islam: Conscience and History in a World Civilization*, 2:3.

11 The later fortunes of the *Rules* and the studies devoted to their various aspects are noted in Street, "Kātibī (d. 1277), Taḥtānī (d. 1365), and the *Shamsiyya*," 365.

12 In Lowry's introduction, quoting Fakhr al-Dīn al-Rāzī's *Irshād al-ṭālibīn ilā l-minhaj al-qawīm fī bayān manāqib al-imām al-Shāfiʿī* (*Guiding Students on the Right Way to Set Out the Virtues of Imām al-Shāfiʿī*); al-Shāfiʿī, *The Epistle on Legal Theory*, xv.

13 Quoted in Gutas, "Aspects of Literary Form and Genre in Arabic Logical Works," 60.

14 Ibn Khaldūn, *The Muqaddimah: An Introduction to History*, 3:142–43.

15 Gutas, "Aspects of Literary Form," 61.

16 Smyth, "Controversy in a Tradition of Commentary: The Academic Legacy of al-Sakkākī's *Miftāḥ al-ʿUlūm*," 594. I take all my information about al-Taftāzānī's relationship with al-Jurjānī from this interesting account.

17 Especially in the modal propositions and the way they contribute to syllogistic inferences; see Street, "Al-ʿAllāma al-Ḥillī (d. 1325) and the Early Reception of Kātibī's *Shamsīya*: Notes towards a Study of the Dynamics of Post-Avicennan Logical Commentary."

18 Described in Tabrīziyān, Introduction to al-Ḥillī, *al-Qawāʿid al-jaliyyah*, 160.

19 Tabrīzī, *Ark of Tabrīz*.

20 Palmer, *A Descriptive Catalogue of the Arabic, Persian, and Turkish Manuscripts in the Library of Trinity College, Cambridge*, 141–43. "Small quarto, 44 pages. Part I. Arabic Nasȟí handwriting, on thick glazed paper, discoloured by age." Part 1, which runs from pages 1b to 28b, contains the *Risālah*. After a lengthy description of the contents of the work, the entry continues: "This copy is said to be an autograph, the following words being written on the first leaf . . . (This is the Risálaȟ Šamsíyaȟ, in the handwriting of its author, the late Mauláná Kátibí); and the appearance of the paper and writing would confirm the statement. An additional proof of its authenticity is that the readings are more correct and intelligible than those of any other MS that I have seen, or those from which the text of Dr. Sprenger and his colleagues was formed . . . A great many marginal notes have been made, in the same handwriting as the following manuscript."

21 Trinity R.13.54. From notes sent by Adam Gacek (to whom I am indebted): *Al-Risālah al-shamsīyah bi-khaṭṭ muṣannifihā mawlānā al-Kātibī ʿalayhi al-raḥmah* (Cambridge Trinity College Arabian Tracts 13) Fol. 1a–28b. Title in calligraphic *thuluth*. No colophon and no date. Script: partly pointed, clear *naskh* with the *nūn* in reverse as in *shikastah*. Assimilated *alif* in the definite article; it looks like ٢. Omissions in the same hand as the body of the text.

22 See, respectively, Tahānawī, *A Dictionary of the Technical Terms Used in the Sciences of the Musalmans*, al-Kātibī, *al-Risālah*, and the 2011 version of al-Taḥtānī, *Taḥrīr*.

23 Faḍlallāh's introduction to the edition of the *Rules* discusses previous printings, 21-22; he names the texts most important for his work and states his editorial goals, 24-25.

24 Bīdārfar names the texts in the introduction to his edition of al-Taḥtānī's *Taḥrīr*, 14.

25 I differ somewhat from the numbering in the Bīdārfar edition; I number the opening dedication as 0 (he has it as 1), and he jumps from 17 (my 16) on page 129 to 19 (my 17) on page 136, so I'm out by one at first, then by two. I suspect the lemmata crystallized as clear-cut and fairly lengthy only in the later nineteenth-century printings of the text. I give a concordance for the lemmata in the Sprenger edition and those in a typical later printing (specifically, a version of the *Taḥrīr* reprinted in Cairo in 1948) in Street, "Kātibī (d. 1277)," 367–72.

26 Rescher, *Temporal Modalities in Arabic Logic.*

27 Rescher and vander Nat, "The Theory of Modal Syllogistic in Medieval Arabic Philosophy."

28 Khaled El-Rouayheb was in the process of preparing an edition of al-Kātibī's *Jāmiʿ al-daqāʾiq*; he has kindly sent me some transcribed text. Qarāmalikī makes use of *al-Munaṣṣaṣ fī sharḥ al-Mulakhkhaṣ* (*The Precise Commentary on the Epitome*), al-Kātibī's commentary on al-Rāzī's *Mulakhkhaṣ* (still in manuscript), and Mohammad Saleh Zarepour transcribed a considerable portion of al-Kātibī's commentary on al-Khūnajī's *Kashf al-asrār* from MS Süleymaniya: Carullah 1417 for a 2018 Cambridge Humanities Research Grant. Since then, a preliminary edition has been given of the whole commentary by Enver Şahin, "Kâtibî'nin Şerhu Keşfi'l-Esrâr Adlı Eserinin Tahkîki ve Değerlendirmesi (Critical Edition and Analysis of Kātibī's Sharh Kashf al-asrâr)," see al-Kātibī, *Sharḥ Kashf al-asrār.*

29 Copenhaver et al., *Peter of Spain: Summaries*; Kilwardby, *Notule libri priorum*; Klima, *John Buridan, Summulae.*

30 Strobino, "Ibn Sina's Logic."

31 See Lameer, *Al-Fārābī and Aristotelian Syllogistics: Greek Theory and Islamic Practice*, 55–62; the story is even more complicated, involving as it does Avicenna's reception of post-Aristotelian commentary, but Lameer's comments are more than enough for present purposes.

الرسالة الشمسيّة في القواعد المنطقيّة

The Rules of Logic

الحمد لله الذي أبدع نظام الوجود واخترع ماهيّات الاشياء بمقتضى الجود وأنشأ بقدرته أنواع الجواهر العقليّة وأفاض برحمته محرّكات الأجرام الفلكيّة والصلاة على ذوات الأنفس القدسيّة المنزّهة عن الكدورات الإنسيّة خصوصاً على سيّدنا محمّد صاحب الآيات والمعجزات وعلى آله وأصحابه التابعين للحجج والبيّنات.

وبعد فلمّا كان باتّفاق أهل العقل وإطباق ذوي الفضل أنّ العلوم سيّما اليقينيّة أعلى المطالب وأبهى المناقب وأنّ صاحبها أشرف الأشخاص البشريّة ونفسه أسرع اتّصالاً بالعقول الملكيّة وكان الاطّلاع على دقائقها والإحاطة بكنه حقائقها لا يمكن إلّا بالعلم الموسوم بالمنطق إذ به تعرف صحّتها من سقمها وغثّها من سمينها فأشار إليّ من سعد بلطف الحقّ وامتاز بتأييده من بين كافّة الخلق ومال إلى جنابه الداني والقاصي وأفلح بمتابعته المطيع والعاصي وهو المولى الصدر الصاحب المعظّم العالم الفاضل المقبول المنعم المحسن الحسيب النسيب ذو المناقب والمفاخر شمس الملّة والدين بهاء الإسلام والمسلمين قدوة الأكابر والأماثل ملك الصدور والأفاضل قطب الأعالي فلك المعالي محمّد بن المولى الصدر المعظّم والصاحب الأعظم دستور الآفاق آصف الزمان ملك وزراء الشرق والغرب صاحب ديوان الممالك بهاء الحقّ والدين ومؤيّد علماء الإسلام والمسلمين قطب الملوك محمد أدام الله ظلالهما وضاعف جلالهما الذي مع حداثة سنّه فاق بالسعادات الأبديّة والكرامات السرمديّة واختصّ بالفضائل الجميلة والخصائل الحميدة بتحرير كتاب في المنطق جامع لقواعده حاوٍ لأصوله وضوابطه فبادرت إلى مقتضى إشارته وشرعت في ثبته وكتابته مستلزماً أن لا أخلّ بشيء يعتدّ به من القواعد والضوابط مع زيادات شريفة ونكت لطيفة من عندي غير تابع لأحد

Praise be to God, who created the system of existence, drew forth the quiddities of things in accordance with His generosity, established through His power the species of intellectual substances, and bestows through His mercy the movements of the celestial bodies. Let us offer prayers for those holy souls free of human stains, especially for Muḥammad, the bringer of signs and miracles, and for his family and companions who follow his arguments and proofs. ٥

The intelligent and the virtuous agree that the sciences—especially the exact sciences—are the highest goal and brightest virtue, and that those proficient in them are the noblest humans, with souls most apt to contact the angelic intelligences. Knowing the subtleties of these sciences and comprehending the essence of the realities they deal with is only possible through the science designated as logic, for by way of it one knows what is correct from what is wrong, what is worthless from what is valuable; knowing this, someone assigned me to compose a book on logic, gathering its rules and containing its principles and guidelines. He who assigned me this task is one who flourishes by the grace of truth, distinguished from all others by its support. Both those close and those distant are drawn to his side, and both the compliant and the wayward thrive through following him, for he is the exalted Lord Master, preeminent, pleasing, beneficent, noble, patrician, possessed of virtue and glorious traits, Sun of the Community, Shams al-Dīn, splendor of Islam and Muslims, model for the great and the exemplary, king of the powerful and the virtuous, pillar of the high, orb of the excellent. He is the son of the exalted and most great Lord Master who governs distant lands, the Asaph of his age,[1] king of ministers from the east and the west, convenor of the imperial court, Splendor of Truth, Bahāʾ al-Dīn, support of the scholars of Islam and of Muslims, pillar of kings. May God lengthen the reach of the power and redouble the glory of both. Though young in years, Shams al-Dīn is crowned with eternal happiness and honor, and characterized by beautiful virtues and praiseworthy traits. He assigned me this task, and I set out to draft the book and write it up, bound by a commitment not to omit any rule or guideline of consequence (along with a

من الخلائق بل للحقّ الصريح الذي ﴿لَا يَأْتِيهِ ٱلْبَٰطِلُ مِنۢ بَيْنِ يَدَيْهِ وَلَا مِنْ خَلْفِهِۦ﴾ وسمّيته بالرسالة الشمسيّة في القواعد المنطقيّة ورتّبته على مقدّمة وثلاث مقالات وخاتمة معتصماً بحبل التوفيق من واهب العقل ومتوكّلاً على جوده المفيض للخير والعدل إنّه خير موفّق ومعين.

few worthy additions and pleasing insights of my own), a commitment not to follow any other logician, but rather plain truth: «falsehood cannot come at it from before it or behind it».[2] I gave this book the title *The Epistle on Logical Rules for Shams al-Dīn*, and I structured it as an Introduction, three Treatises, and a Conclusion; clinging all the while to the lifeline given by the Giver of Intellect,[3] and relying on His generosity, which bestows goodness and justice. Indeed, He is the best of those who sustain and grant aid.

أمّا المقدّمة

ففيها بحثان

الأوّل في ماهيّة المنطق وبيان الحاجة إليه

العلم إمّا تصوّر فقط وهو حصول صورة الشيء في العقل أو تصوّر معه حكم وهو ١
إسناد أمر إلى آخر إيجاباً أو سلباً ويقال للمجموع تصديق.

وليس الكلّ من كلّ منهما بديهيّاً وإلّا لما جهلنا شيئاً ولا نظريّاً وإلّا لدار أو ٢
تسلسل.

بل البعض من كلّ منهما بديهيّ والبعض نظريّ يحصل بالفكر وهو ترتيب أمور ٣
معلومة للتأدّي بها إلى المجهول وذلك الترتيب ليس بصواب دائماً لمناقضة بعض العقلاء بعضاً في مقتضى أفكارهم بل الإنسان الواحد يناقض نفسه في وقتين مختلفين فمسّت الحاجة إلى قانون يفيد معرفة طرق اكتساب النظريّات من الضروريّات والإحاطة بالصحيح والفاسد من الفكر الواقع فيها وهو المنطق ورسموه بأنّه آلة قانونيّة تعصم مراعاتُها الذهن عن الخطأ في الفكر.

وليس كلّه بديهيّاً وإلّا لاستُغنِيَ عن تعلّمه ولا نظريّاً وإلّا لدار أو تسلسل بل بعضه ٤
بديهيّ وبعضه نظريّ يستفاد منه.

The Introduction

Containing two discussions

The First Discussion: On the Quiddity of Logic, and Proof of the Need for It

Knowledge is either merely conception, which is the occurrence of the form of something in the intellect, or conception together with a judgment, which is the subordination of one thing to another affirmatively or negatively; such an aggregate of conception and judgment is called assertion. 1

It is not the case that the whole of each of the two divisions of knowledge is entirely primitive (otherwise there would be nothing we do not know) or entirely inferred (otherwise knowledge claims would form a vicious circle or regress). 2

Rather, part of each division of knowledge is primitive, and part inferred, obtained by thinking, which is the ordering of known things such that they lead to knowledge of the unknown. But this ordering is not always correct, given that some thinkers contradict others according to what they think and, indeed, the same person may contradict himself at different times. Thus, there is need for a canon that provides knowledge of the ways of acquiring inferred knowledge from necessary propositions, and that also provides the comprehension of sound and unsound thinking which arises in the course of such acquisition—this is logic. It is delineated as a canonical instrument, which, if implemented, preserves our mind from error in thinking. 3

Logic is neither entirely primitive (otherwise we could dispense with learning it), nor is it entirely inferred (otherwise its claims would form a vicious circle or regress); but part of it is primitive, and part inferred from what is primitive. 4

البحث الثاني في موضوع المنطق

٥ موضوع كلّ علم ما يبحث فيه عن عوارضه الذاتيّة التي تلحقه لما هو هو أي لذاته أو لما يساويه أو لجزئه وموضوع المنطق المعلومات التصوّريّة والتصديقيّة لأنّ المنطقيّ يبحث عنها من حيث أنّها توصل إلى تصوّر أو تصديق ومن حيث يتوقّف عليها الموصل إلى التصوّر ككونها كلّيّة وجزئيّة وذاتيّة وعرضيّة وجنساً وفصلاً ومن حيث يتوقّف عليها الموصل إلى التصديق إمّا توقّفاً قريباً ككونها قضيّة وعكس قضيّة ونقيض قضيّة وإمّا توقّفاً بعيداً ككونها موضوعات ومحمولات.

٦ وقد جرت العادة بأن يسمّى الموصل إلى التصوّر قولاً شارحاً والموصل إلى التصديق حجّة ويجب تقديم الأوّل على الثاني وضعاً لتقدّم التصوّر على التصديق طبعاً لأنّ كلّ تصديق لا بدّ له من تصوّر المحكوم عليه بذاته أو بأمر صادق عليه والمحكوم به كذلك والحكم لامتناع الحكم ممّن جهل أحد هذه الأشياء.

The Second Discussion: On the Subject of Logic

The subject of a science is that whose essential accidents are investigated in the 5
science, accidents that attach to the subject due to what it is (that is, due to its essence), or due to what is coextensive with it, or a part of it. So the subject of logic is known conceptions and assertions, because the logician investigates them insofar as they conduce to a conception or an assertion. He also investigates them insofar as what conduces to conception depends on them, like their being universal, particular, essential, accidental, genus, or differentia; and insofar as what conduces to assertion depends on them, whether proximately (like their being a proposition, the converse of a proposition, the contradictory of a proposition) or remotely (like their being subject and predicate).

It is customary to call what conduces to conception an explanatory phrase, 6
and to call what conduces to assertion an argument. The first must be put before the second in an exposition due to the priority by nature of conception over assertion. This is because every assertion must involve the conception of what is subject to judgment (whether in itself, or under a matter that happens to be true of it); then, likewise, of what is judged to belong to it; and, finally, of the judgment itself, because it is impossible for anyone who is ignorant of any of these things to make a judgment.

وأمّا المقالات فثلاث

المقالة الأولى في المفردات

وفيها أربعة فصول

الفصل الأوّل في الألفاظ

٧ دلالة اللفظ على المعنى بتوسّط الوضع له مطابقة كدلالة الإنسان على الحيوان الناطق وبتوسّطه لما دخل فيه تضمّن كدلالته على الحيوان أو الناطق وبتوسّطه لما خرج عنه التزام كدلالته على قابل صنعة الكتابة.

٨ ويُشترط في الدلالة الالتزاميّة كون الخارج بحالة يلزم من تصوّر المسمّى تصوّره وإلّا لامتنع فهمه من اللفظ ولا يُشترط فيها كونه بحالة يلزم من تحقّق المسمّى في الخارج تحقّقه كدلالة لفظ العمى على البصر مع عدم الملازمة بينهما في الخارج.

٩ والمطابقة لا تستلزم التضمّن كما في البسائط وأمّا استلزامها الالتزام فغير متيقّن لأنّ وجود لازم لكلّ ماهيّة يلزم من تصوّرها تصوّره غير معلوم وما قيل إنّ تصوّر كلّ ماهيّة يستلزم تصوّر أنّها ليست غيرها ممنوع ومن هذا تبيّن عدم استلزام التضمّن الالتزام وأمّا هما فلا يوجدان بدون المطابقة لاستحالة وجود التابع من حيث أنّه تابع بدون المتبوع.

There are three treatises:

The First Treatise: On Simple Terms

Containing four sections

The First Section: On Expressions

7 The expression's signification of a meaning by way of its having been imposed on that meaning is correspondence; this is like "man" signifying rational animal. The expression's signifying by way of that imposition what is contained in its meaning by correspondence is containment; this is like "man" signifying animal or rational. The expression's signifying by way of that imposition what is extrinsic to its meaning by correspondence is implication; this is like "man" signifying receptive of skill in writing.[4]

8 It is stipulated for implicational signification that the extrinsic implicate be such that its conception follow from the conception of the named; otherwise, its being understood from the expression would be impossible. It is not, however, stipulated that the implicate be such that its actual realization follow from the actual realization of the named. This is like the expression "blind," which signifies sight even though there is no implicational relation between the two in actual existence.

9 Correspondence does not entail containment, as emerges when considering the case of simple entities. Whether correspondence entails implication is not known for sure, because it is unknowable whether there is a mental implicate belonging to every quiddity whose conception follows from the conception of that quiddity. We have ruled out what has been said, that the conception of every quiddity entails the conception that it is not other than itself. From this it would also be clear that containment does not entail implication. Containment and implication only come about with correspondence, due to the impossibility of a consequent—insofar as it is a consequent—without an antecedent.

١٠ والدالّ بالمطابقة إن قُصد بجزئه الدلالة على جزء معناه فهو المركّب كرامي الحجارة وإلّا فهو المفرد.

١١ وهو إن لم يصلح لأن يخبر به فهو الأداة كفي ولا وإن صلح لذلك فإن دلّ بهيئته على زمان معيّن من الأزمنة الثلاثة فهو الكلمة وإن لم يدلّ فهو الاسم.

١،١٢ وحينئذ إمّا أن يكون معناه واحداً أو كثيراً فإن كان الأوّل فإن تشخّص ذلك المعنى سمّي عَلَماً وإلّا فمتواطئاً إن استوت أفراده الذهنيّة والخارجيّة فيه كالإنسان والشمس ومشكّكاً إن كان حصوله في البعض أولى وأقدم من الآخر كالوجود بالنسبة إلى الواجب والممكن.

٢،١٢ وإن كان الثاني فإن كان وضعه لتلك المعاني على السويّة فهو المشترك كالعين وإن لم يكن كذلك بل وُضع لأحدهما ثمّ نُقل إلى الثاني وحينئذ إن تُرك موضوعه الأوّل يسمّى منقولاً عرفيّاً إن كان الناقل هو العرف العامّ كالدابّة وشرعيّاً إن كان هو الشارع كالصلاة والصوم واصطلاحيّاً إن كان هو العرف الخاصّ كاصطلاحات النحاة والنظّار.

٣،١٢ وإن لم يُترك موضوعه الأوّل يسمّى بالنسبة إليه حقيقة وبالنسبة إلى المنقول إليه مجازاً كالأسد بالنسبة إلى الحيوان المفترس والرجل الشجاع.

١٣ وكلّ لفظ فهو بالنسبة إلى لفظ آخر مرادف له إن توافقا في المعنى ومباين له إن اختلفا فيه.

١،١٤ وأمّا المركّب فهو إمّا تامّ وهو الذي يصحّ عليه السكوت وإمّا غير تامّ وهو الذي يقابله.

٢،١٤ والتامّ إن احتمل الصدق والكذب فهو الخبر وإن لم يحتمل فإن دلّ على طلب الفعل دلالة أوّليّة أي وضعيّة فهو مع الاستعلاء أمر كقولنا اضرب ومع الخضوع

10 If one intends to signify by part of what signifies through correspondence a part of its meaning, then it is a compound expression (like "stone-thrower"); otherwise, it is a simple expression.

11 If the expression is not fit to be a predicate, it is a particle, like "in" and "not." If it is fit to be a predicate, then if by its form it signifies one of the three tenses specifically, it is a verb. If it does not so signify, it is a name.[5]

12.1 Thereupon, its meaning is either one or many. If it is the first, then if that meaning is for an individual, it is a proper name. Otherwise, if its members—both mental and actual—are equal under it, as with "man" and "sun," it is univocal. But if its occurrence in one is more eminent than, and prior to, the other—like existence in relation to the necessary and the contingent—then it is systematically ambiguous.

12.2 If it is the second, with many meanings, then if it is imposed equally on each of those meanings, it is equivocal, like *ʿayn*.[6] If that is not the case, but rather it has been imposed in the first place on one of the two meanings, and then transferred to the second such that its first imposition has been abandoned, then it is called a conventionally transferred expression if it is transferred by general convention, as in the case of the word *dābbah*, "animal," which has come to mean "mount"; it is called a legislatively transferred expression if it is transferred by revealed legislation, as in the case of the word *ṣalāt*, "prayer," which has come to mean "ritual prayer," and the word *ṣawm*, "fasting," which has come to mean "ritual fasting"; and it is called a technically transferred expression if it is transferred by special convention, as in the case of the technical usage of the grammarians and theorists.

12.3 If the primary imposition has not been abandoned, the expression is said to be literal in relation to what it was initially imposed upon, and figurative in relation to what it has been transferred to, like "lion" in relation to the wild animal and the courageous man.[7]

13 Every expression, when taken in relation to another expression, is synonymous with it if the two agree in meaning, and distinct from it if they differ.[8]

14.1 A compound expression is either complete (after which silence is appropriate) or incomplete (which is the opposite).

14.2 If a complete expression bears the valuations true and false, it is information. But if it does not, then, if as its primary (that is, its imposed) signification it signifies seeking that an action be undertaken, it is a command (like "Beat!") when said with haughtiness; with submissiveness, a petition and

سؤال ودعاء ومع التساوي التماس وإن لم يدلّ فهو التنبيه ويندرج فيه التمنّي والترجّي والقسم والنداء.

وأمّا غير التامّ فهو إمّا تقييديّ كالحيوان الناطق وإمّا غير تقييديّ كالمركّب من ٣،١٤
اسم وأداة أو كلمة وأداة.

الفصل الثاني في المعاني المفردة

كلّ مفهوم فهو جزئيّ حقيقيّ إن منع نفس تصوّر معناه من وقوع الشركة فيه وكلّيّ ١٥
إن لم يمنع واللفظ الدالّ عليهما يسمّى جزئيّاً وكلّيّاً بالعرض.

والكلّيّ إمّا أن يكون تمام ماهيّة ما تحته من الجزئيّات أو داخلاً فيها أو خارجاً ١،١٦
عنها.

والأوّل هو النوع الحقيقيّ سواء كان متعدّد الأشخاص وهو المقول في جواب ما هو ٢،١٦
بحسب الشركة والخصوصيّة معاً كالإنسان أو غير متعدّد الأشخاص وهو المقول في جواب ما هو بحسب الخصوصيّة المحضة كالشمس فهو إذن كلّيّ مقول على واحد أو على كثيرين متّفقين بالحقائق في جواب ما هو.

وإن كان الثاني فإن كان تمام الجزء المشترك بينها وبين نوع آخر فهو المقول في جواب ١٧
ما هو بحسب الشركة المحضة ويسمّى جنساً ورسموه بأنّه الكلّيّ المقول على كثيرين مختلفين بالحقائق في جواب ما هو.

وهو قريب إن كان الجواب عن الماهيّة وعن بعض ما يشاركها فيه هو الجواب عنها ١،١٨
وعن كلّ ما يشاركها فيه كالحيوان بالنسبة إلى الإنسان وبعيد إن كان الجواب عنها وعن بعض ما يشاركها فيه غير الجواب عنها وعن البعض الآخر.

supplication; with equality, a request. If it does not signify any of these, it is a notification, under which are subsumed wishing, hoping, oath swearing, and calling.

An incomplete expression is either restrictive, like "rational animal," or nonrestrictive, like the compound of a name and a particle, or a verb with a particle. 14.3

The Second Section: On Simple Meanings

Every concept is a real particular if the very conception of its meaning precludes sharing in the meaning, and universal if the conception of its meaning does not preclude such sharing. The expression signifying one or the other kind of meaning is said to be particular or universal per accidens. 15

The universal is either the whole quiddity of the particulars under it, or intrinsic to the quiddity, or extrinsic from it. 16.1

The first division—that is, the whole quiddity—is the real species, whether it has numerous individuals under it (and this universal is what is said in answer to the question "what is it?" in respect of both sharing and specificity, like man) or does not have numerous individuals under it (and this universal is what is said in answer to the question "what is it?" in respect of pure specificity, like sun). Thus, the real species is a universal said of one or of many things, which agree in realities in answer to the question "what is it?"[9] 16.2

If it is the second division—that is, something intrinsic to the quiddity—if it is the whole of the part shared between the quiddity and another species, then this is what is said in answer to the question "what is it?" in respect of pure sharing, and is called genus. They delineate this universal as a universal said of many, which differ in realities in answer to the question "what is it?" 17

The genus is proximate if the answer about the quiddity and about something that shares with the quiddity in the putatively proximate genus is the same as the answer about the quiddity and about whatever else shares with it in that genus, like animal in relation to man. The genus is remote if the answer about the quiddity and about something that shares with it in the putatively remote genus is not the same as the answer about the quiddity and something else under the genus. 18.1

٢،١٨ ويكون هناك جوابان إن كان بعيداً بمرتبة واحدة كالجسم النامي بالنسبة إلى الإنسان وثلاثة أجوبة إن كان بعيداً بمرتبتين كالجسم وأربعة أجوبة إن كان بعيداً بثلاث مراتب وعلى هذا القياس.

١٩ وإن لم يكن تمام المشترك بينها وبين نوع آخر فلا بدّ وأن لا يكون مشتركاً أو بعضاً من تمام المشترك مساوياً له وإلّا لكان مشتركاً بين الماهيّة وبين نوع آخر ولا يجوز أن يكون تمام[١] المشترك بالنسبة إلى ذلك النوع لأنّ المقدّر خلافه بل بعضه ولا يتسلسل بل ينتهي إلى ما يساويه فيكون فصل جنس وكيف كان يميّز الماهيّة عن مشاركها في جنس أو وجود فكان فصلاً.

٢٠ ورسموه بأنّه كلّيّ يُحمل على الشيء في جواب أيّ شيء هو في جوهره فعلى هذا لو تركّبت حقيقة من أمرين متساويين أو أمور متساوية كان كلّ منها فصلاً لها لأنّه يميّزها عن مشاركها في الوجود.

٢١ والفصل المميّز للنوع عن مشاركه في الجنس قريب إن ميّزه عنه في جنس قريب كالناطق للإنسان وبعيد إن ميّزه عنه في جنس بعيد كالحسّاس للإنسان.

١،٢٢ وأمّا الثالث فإن امتنع انفكاكه عن معروضه فهو اللازم وإلّا فهو العرضيّ المفارق.[٢]

٢،٢٢ واللازم قد يكون لازماً للوجود كالسواد للحبشيّ وقد يكون لازماً للماهيّة وهو إمّا بيّن وهو الذي يكون تصوّره مع تصوّر ملزومه كافياً في جزم الذهن باللزوم بينهما كالانقسام بمتساويين للأربعة وإمّا غير بيّن وهو الذي يفتقر جزم الذهن باللزوم بينهما إلى وسط كتساوي زوايا المثلّث للقائمتين وقد يقال البيّن على اللازم الذي يلزم من تصوّر ملزومه تصوّره والأوّل أعمّ.

٣،٢٢ والعرضيّ إمّا سريع الزوال كحمرة الخجل وصفرة الوجل وإمّا بطيؤه كالشيب والشباب.

١ (تمام) في ر، س، ف، ك؛ ساقطة من ت. ٢ (العرضيّ المفارق) في س، ك؛ ت، ر، ف: العرض المفارق.

There are two answers to "what is it?" if it is remote by one degree (like growing body in relation to man), three answers if it is remote by two degrees (like body), four answers if it is remote by three degrees, and so on like this.[10] 18.2

If it is not the whole part that is shared between the quiddity and another species, then inevitably either it is not shared, or it is a part of the whole that is shared and coextensive with it. Otherwise, it would be shared between the quiddity and another species. Yet it cannot be the whole that is shared in relation to that species, because the hypothesis is to the contrary. Rather, it is part of what is shared. This does not regress ad infinitum, but rather terminates in what is coextensive with what is shared, so it is the differentia of a genus. No matter how it distinguishes the quiddity from what shares with it—whether in a genus or in existence—it is a differentia. 19

They delineate the differentia as a universal predicated of something in answer to the question "which thing is it?" with respect to its substance. On this account, were a reality compounded from two or more coextensive matters, then each one would be a differentia for the reality, because each would distinguish it from what shares with it in existence. 20

The differentia distinguishing the species from what shares with it in genus is proximate if it distinguishes the species from what shares with it in a proximate genus (like "rational" for man), and remote if it distinguishes the species from what shares with it in a remote genus (like "sensate" for man). 21

As for the third division (in which the universal is extrinsic from the quiddity of the particulars under it),[11] if it is impossible to separate it from its substrate then it is an implicate; otherwise, it is a separable accidental. 22.1

The implicate may be an implicate of the existence of something, like black for the Ethiopian, and it may be an implicate of the quiddity. It is either evident, such that its conception along with the conception of its implicant is sufficient for the mind to declare an implication between the two (like divisibility into two equal parts for four); or it is not evident, such that it needs a middle for the mind to declare that there is an implication between the two (like the three angles of triangle summing to two right angles). "Evident" may also be said of an implicate whose conception follows from the conception of its implicant; the first definition is the more general.[12] 22.2

The separable accidental may disappear quickly, like the redness of a blush or the pallor of fear; or it may do so slowly, like the graying of hair or the passing of youth. 22.3

٢٣ وكلّ واحد من اللازم والمفارق إن اختصّ بأفراد حقيقة واحدة فهو الخاصّة كالضاحك وإلّا فهو العرض العامّ كالماشي وترسم الخاصّة بأنّها كلّيّة مقولة على ما تحت حقيقة واحدة فقط قولاً عرضيّاً والعرض العامّ بأنّه كلّيّ مقول على أفراد حقيقة واحدة وغيرها قولاً عرضيّاً فالكلّيّات إذن خمسة نوع وجنس وفصل وخاصّة وعرض عامّ.

الفصل الثالث في مباحث الكلّيّ والجزئيّ وهي خمسة

٢٤ الأوّل الكلّيّ قد يكون ممتنع الوجود في الخارج لا لنفس مفهوم اللفظ كشريك البارئ عزّ اسمه وقد يكون ممكن الوجود لكن لا يوجد كالعنقاء وقد يكون الموجود منه واحداً فقط مع امتناع غيره كالبارئ تعالى أو مع إمكانه كالشمس وقد يكون الموجود منه كثيراً إمّا متناهياً كالكواكب السبعة السيّارة أو غير متناه كالنفوس الناطقة.

٢٥ الثاني إذا قلنا للحيوان مثلاً إنّه كلّيّ فهناك أمور ثلاثة الحيوان من حيث هو هو وكونه كلّيّاً والمركّب منهما والأوّل يسمّى كلّيّاً طبيعيّاً والثاني كلّيّاً منطقيّاً والثالث كلّيّاً عقليّاً والكلّيّ الطبيعيّ موجود في الخارج لأنّه جزء من هذا الحيوان الموجود في الخارج وجزء الموجود موجود وأمّا الكلّيّان الآخران ففي وجودهما في الخارج خلاف والنظر فيهما خارج عن المنطق.

٢٦ الثالث الكلّيّان متساويان إن صدق كلّ منهما على كلّ ما صدق عليه الآخر كالإنسان والناطق وبينهما عموم مطلق إن صدق أحدهما على كلّ ما صدق عليه الآخر من غير عكس كالحيوان والإنسان وبينهما عموم من وجه إن صدق كلّ منهما

If either the implicate or the separable is possessed solely by the members of one reality, it is a proprium (like "laughing"); otherwise, it is a general accident (like "walking"). We delineate the proprium as a universal said in an accidental way of what is under a single reality only, and general accident as a universal said in an accidental way of members of more than one reality. The universals are therefore five: species, genus, differentia, proprium, and general accident. 23

The Third Section: On Universals and Particulars

Containing five discussions

The First Discussion It may be that the universal cannot possibly exist outside the mind, though not due to the meaning of the expression alone, like partner of the Creator; and it may possibly exist yet not actually exist, like phoenix; and it may be that the existent under it is only one, and no other is possible, like the Creator; or that the existent under it is only one, but it is possible for there to be another, like sun; and it may be that there are many existents under it, whether finite (like the seven planets) or infinite (like rational souls).[13] 24

The Second Discussion If we say of animal, for example, that it is a universal, there are three aspects to this: animal insofar as it is what it is, its being a universal, and the compound of the two. The first is called a natural universal, the second a logical universal, and the third a mental universal. The natural universal exists outside the mind because it is a part of this actually existent animal, and a part of an existent is existent. There is dispute about whether the other two universals exist outside the mind, but investigation into them falls outside logic. 25

The Third Discussion Two universals are coextensive if each one is true of whatever the other is true of, like man and rational. One is included within the other if one is true of whatever the other is true of, without the converse being the case, like animal and man. The two overlap if each one is only true of part of what the other is true of, like animal and white. And they 26

على بعض ما صدق عليه الآخر كالحيوان والأبيض ومتباينان إن لم يصدق شيء منهما على شيء مما صدق عليه الآخر كالإنسان والفرس.

١،٢٧ ونقيضا المتساويين متساويان وإلّا لصدق أحدهما على ما كذب عليه الآخر فصدق أحد المتساويين على ما كذب عليه الآخر وهو محال.

٢،٢٧ ونقيض الأعمّ من شيء مطلقاً أخصّ من نقيض الأخصّ مطلقاً لصدق نقيض الأخصّ على كلّ ما صدق عليه نقيض الأعمّ من غير عكس أمّا الأوّل فلأنّه لو لا ذلك لصدق عين الأخصّ على بعض ما صدق عليه نقيض الأعمّ وذلك مستلزم لصدق الأخصّ بدون الأعمّ وهو محال وأمّا الثاني فلأنّه لو لا ذلك لصدق نقيض الأعمّ على كلّ ما يصدق عليه نقيض الأخصّ وذلك مستلزم لصدق الأخصّ على كلّ ما يصدق عليه الأعمّ وهو محال.

٣،٢٧ والأعمّ من شيء من وجه ليس بين نقيضيهما عموم أصلاً لتحقّق مثل هذا العموم بين عين الأعمّ مطلقاً وبين نقيض الأخصّ مع التباين الكلّيّ بين نقيض الأعمّ مطلقاً وعين الأخصّ.

٤،٢٧ ونقيضا المتباينين متباينان تباينا جزئيّاً لأنّهما إن لم يصدقا كاللاوجود واللاعدم كان بينهما تباين كلّيّ وإن صدقا كاللاإنسان واللافرس كان بينهما تباين جزئيّ ضرورة صدق أحد المتباينين مع نقيض الآخر فقط فالتباين الجزئيّ لازم جزماً.

٢٨ الرابع الجزئيّ كما يقال على المعنى المذكور المسمّى بالحقيقي فكذلك يقال على كلّ أخصّ تحت الأعمّ ويسمّى الجزئيّ الإضافيّ وهو أعمّ من الأوّل لأنّ كلّ جزئيّ حقيقيّ فهو جزئيّ إضافيّ بدون العكس أمّا الأوّل فلاندراج كلّ شخص تحت ماهيّته المعرّاة

are disjunct if neither is true of anything of which the other is true, like man and horse.[14]

The contradictories of two coextensive universals are coextensive. Were that not the case, then one of the two contradictories would be true of what the other is false of, so one of the original coextensive universals would be true of what the other is false of, and that is inconceivable. 27.1

In the case of inclusion, the contradictory of the more general simpliciter is more specific than the contradictory of the more specific simpliciter, due to the fact that the contradictory of the more specific is true of everything of which the contradictory of the more general is true, though not the reverse. As for the first part of the claim, it is because, were that not the case, then the more specific itself would be true of some of what the contradictory of the more general is true of, and that entails the truth of the more specific without the more general, and that is inconceivable. As for the second part of the claim, it is because, were that not the case, the contradictory of the more general would be true of everything of which the contradictory of the more specific is true, and that entails that the more specific be true of all of the more general, and that is inconceivable. 27.2

As for universals that overlap, there is no fundamental reason their two contradictories should overlap, due to the verification of the like of this limited overlap between the more general simpliciter and the contradictory of the more specific, along with complete disjunction between the contradictory of the more general simpliciter and the more specific itself. 27.3

The two contradictories of two disjuncts are disjoined at least partly. This is because if the two taken together are not true of anything—like nonexistence and non-privation—there is a complete disjunction between the two. And if they can be true together—like not-man and not-horse—there is a partial disjunction between the two as a necessary consequence of the fact that one of the two disjuncts is true only with the contradictory of the other. So partial disjunction is certainly an implicate in this case.[15] 27.4

The Fourth Discussion Just as "particular" is said of the meaning mentioned above (what is termed the real particular),[16] it is likewise said of everything more specific under the more general. This is called the relative particular, and it is more general than the first, because every real particular is a relative 28

عن المشخّصات وأمّا الثاني فلجواز كون الجزئيّ الإضافيّ كلّيًا وامتناع كون الجزئيّ الحقيقيّ كذلك.

٢٩ الخامس النوع كما يقال على ما ذكرناه ويقال له النوع الحقيقيّ فكذلك يقال على كلّ ماهيّة يقال عليها وعلى غيرها الجنس في جواب ما هو قولاً أوّليًا ويسمّى النوع الإضافيّ.

٣٠ ومراتبه أربع لأنّه إمّا أعمّ الأنواع وهو النوع العالي كالجسم أو أخصّها وهو النوع السافل كالإنسان ويسمّى نوع الأنواع[١] أو أعمّ من السافل وأخصّ من العالي وهو النوع المتوسّط كالحيوان والجسم النامي أو مباين للكلّ وهو النوع المفرد كالعقل إن قلنا إنّ الجوهر جنس.

٣١ ومراتب الأجناس أيضاً هذه الأربع لكنّ الجنس العالي كالجوهر في مراتب الأجناس يسمّى جنس الأجناس لا السافل كالحيوان ومثال المتوسّط فيها الجسم النامي والجسم ومثال المفرد[٢] العقل إن قلنا إنّ الجوهر ليس بجنس.

٣٢ والنوع الإضافيّ موجود بدون الحقيقيّ كالأنواع المتوسّطة والحقيقيّ موجود بدون الإضافيّ كالحقائق البسيطة فليس بينهما عموم وخصوص مطلق بل كلّ منهما[٣] أعمّ من الآخر من وجه[٤] لصدقهما على النوع السافل.

٣٣ وجزء المقول في جواب ما هو إن كان مذكوراً بالمطابقة يسمّى واقعاً في طريق ما هو كالحيوان والناطق بالنسبة إلى الحيوان الناطق المقول في جواب السؤال بما هو عن الإنسان وإن كان مذكوراً بالتضمّن يسمّى داخلاً في جواب ما هو كالجسم النامي والحسّاس والمتحرّك بالإرادة الدالّ عليها الحيوان بالتضمّن.

٣٤ والجنس العالي جاز أن يكون له فصل يقوّمه لجواز تركّبه من أمرين متساويين[٥] أو من أمور متساوية ويجب أن يكون له فصل يقسّمه والنوع السافل يجب أن يكون له

١ (أو أخصّها. . . نوع الأنواع) في ر، س، ف، ك؛ ساقطة من ت. ٢ (ومثال المفرد): في ك؛ ت، ر: الجس المفرد. ٣ (منهما) في ر، س، ف، ك؛ ت: منها. ٤ (من وجه) في ر، س، ف، ك؛ ساقطة من ت. ٥ (متساويين) في ر، س، ف، ك؛ ساقطة من ت.

particular, without the converse being the case. As for the first part of the claim, it is because every individual is subsumed by its quiddity stripped of whatever individuates it; as for the second, it is because the relative particular can be a universal, whereas the real particular cannot.

The Fifth Discussion Just as "species" is said of what we mentioned above (what is termed the real species),[17] it may likewise be said of every quiddity that, along with other quiddities, has a genus said of it as a primary response to the question "what is it?" This is called relative species. 29

The ranks of relative species come to four: it is either the most general of the species, which is the supreme species, like body; or the most specific of them, which is the inferior species, like man (and it is called the species of species); or more general than the inferior and more specific than the supreme, which is the intermediate species, like animal and growing body; or distinct from everything else, which is the isolated species, like intelligence (if it is said that substance is a genus for it). 30

The ranks of genera also come to these four, but the supreme rank of the ranks of genera (like substance)—and not the inferior (like animal)—is called the genus of genera; an example of an intermediate genus is growing body and body; and an example of the isolated is intelligence (if we say substance is not a genus for it). 31

We may find the relative species without the real species (as in the case of the intermediate species), and the real without the relative (as in the case of the simple realities). One is therefore not included in the other; rather, the two overlap because both are true of the inferior species. 32

Part of what is said in answer to "what is it?," if it is said by correspondence, is called what arises on the way to "what is it?"; this is like animal and rational in relation to "rational animal" said in response to the question "what is it?" asked about man. If it is mentioned by containment, it is called intrinsic to the answer to "what is it?"; this is like body and growing and sensate and moving voluntarily, which "animal" signifies by containment. 33

The superior genus may have a differentia that constitutes it (because the genus may be compounded from two or more coextensive matters), and it must have a differentia that divides it. The inferior species must have a differentia that constitutes it, and cannot have a differentia that divides it. The intermediates must have differentiae that constitute them and 34

فصل يقوّمه ويمتنع أن يكون له فصل يقسّمه والمتوسّطات يجب أن يكون لها فصول تقوّمها وفصول تقسّمها وكلّ فصل يقوّم العالي فهو يقوّم السافل من غير عكس كلّيّ وكلّ فصل يقسّم السافل فهو يقسّم العالي من غير عكس كلّيّ.

الفصل الرابع في التعريفات

٣٥ المعرِّف للشيء هو الذي يستلزم تصوّره تصوّر ذلك الشيء أو امتيازه عن كلّ ما عداه وهو لا يجوز أن يكون نفس الماهيّة لأنّ المعرِّف معلوم قبل المعرَّف والشيء لا يُعلم قبل نفسه ولا أعمّ لقصوره عن إفادة التعريف ولا أخصّ لكونه أخفى فهو مساو لها في العموم والخصوص.

٣٦ ويسمّى حدّاً تامّاً إن كان بالجنس والفصل القريبين وحدّاً ناقصاً إن كان بالفصل القريب وحده أو به وبالجنس البعيد ورسماً تامّاً إن كان بالجنس القريب والخاصّة ورسماً ناقصاً إن كان بالخاصّة وحدها أو بها وبالجنس البعيد.

١،٣٧ ويجب الاحتراز عن تعريف الشيء بما يساويه في المعرفة والجهالة كتعريف الحركة بما ليس بساكن والزوج بما ليس بفرد وعن تعريف الشيء بما لا يُعرف إلّا به سواء كان بمرتبة واحدة كما يقال الكيفيّة ما بها تقع المشابهة ثمّ يقال المشابهة اتّفاق في الكيفيّة أو بمراتب كما يقال الاثنان زوج أوّل ثمّ يقال الزوج هو المنقسم بمتساويين ثمّ يقال المتساويان هما الشيئان اللذان لا يفضل أحدهما على الآخر ثمّ يقال الشيئان هما الاثنان.

٢،٣٧ ويجب أن يُحترز عن استعمال ألفاظ غريبة وحشيّة غير ظاهرة الدلالة بالقياس إلى السائل لكونه مفوّتاً للغرض.

differentiae that divide them. Every differentia that constitutes the superior constitutes the inferior, though this does not convert universally. Every differentia that divides the inferior divides the superior, though this does not convert universally.

The Fourth Section: On Definitions

What defines a given thing is something that, when it is conceived, entails the conception of that thing, or that thing's distinction from everything else. The definition may not be the quiddity itself, because the definition is known prior to what is made known, and a thing is not known prior to itself; nor may it be more general than what is defined (otherwise it would fall short of conveying a definition); nor may it be more specific (otherwise it would be more obscure than what is to be defined). The definition must be coextensive with what is being defined. 35

It is called a complete definition if it is by way of the proximate genus and differentia, and an incomplete definition if it comes about through the proximate differentia alone, or through the proximate differentia and the remote genus. It is called complete delineation if it comes about through the proximate genus and the proprium, and incomplete delineation if it comes about through the proprium alone, or through the proprium and the remote genus.[18] 36

One must be careful not to define something by what is equally known or unknown, as in defining "motion" by "what is not at rest," or "even" by "what is not odd." Nor may one thing be defined by another that is known only through the first, whether at one remove (as in "Quality is that in which similarity occurs," then "Similarity is coincidence in quality"), or at several removes (as in, "2 is the first even," then "the even is divisible into two equal parts," then "two equal parts are two things neither of which exceeds the other," then "two things are 2"). 37.1

One must be careful not to use strange and barbarous expressions, which will be—in relation to the questioner—unclear as to what they signify. This would be to miss the whole purpose of the exercise. 37.2

المقالة الثانية في القضايا وأحكامها

وفيها مقدّمة وثلاثة فصول

أمّا المقدّمة ففي تعريف القضيّة وأقسامها الأوّليّة

٣٨ القضيّة قول يصحّ أن يقال لقائله إنّه صادق أوكاذب وهي حمليّة إن انحلّت بطرفيها إلى مفردين كقولنا زيد عالم زيد ليس بعالم وشرطيّة إن لم تنحلّ.

٣٩ والشرطيّة إمّا متّصلة وهي التي يُحكم فيها بصدق قضيّة أو لا صدقها على تقدير أخرى[1] كقولنا إن كان هذا إنسانًا فهو حيوان وليس إن كان هذا إنسانًا فهو جماد وإمّا منفصلة وهي التي يُحكم فيها بالتنافي بين قضيّتين في الصدق والكذب معًا أو في أحدهما فقط أو بنفيه كقولنا إمّا أن يكون هذا العدد زوجًا أو فردًا وليس إمّا أن يكون الإنسان حيوانًا أو أسود.

الفصل الأوّل في الحمليّة

وفيه أربعة مباحث

٤٠ الأوّل في أجزائها وأقسامها الحمليّة إنّما تتحقّق بأجزاء ثلاثة محكوم عليه ويسمّى موضوعًا ومحكوم به ويسمّى محمولًا ونسبة بينهما بها يرتبط المحمول بالموضوع واللفظ الدالّ عليها يسمّى رابطة كهو في قولنا زيد هو عالم وتسمّى القضيّة حينئذ ثلاثيّة وقد تُحذف الرابطة في بعض اللغات لشعور الذهن بمعناها والقضيّة حينئذ تسمّى ثنائيّة.

---

١ (على تقدير أخرى) في ر، س، ك؛ ت :على تقدير صدق أخرى.

The Second Treatise: On Propositions and Their Valuations

Containing an introduction and three sections

The Introduction: On Defining the Proposition and Its Primary Divisions

A proposition is a discourse such that it is correct to say of him who produces it that he is truthful or false in what he says. It is a categorical proposition if its two extremes may be analyzed into two simple terms, as in "Zayd is knowing," or "Zayd is not knowing"; it is hypothetical if it cannot be analyzed in such a way.[19] 38

The hypothetical proposition is either conditional or disjunctive. A conditional is that in which one proposition is judged to be true or not on the assumption of another proposition. This is like "if this is a man, it is an animal," and "not, if this is a man, it is inanimate." A disjunctive is that in which two propositions are judged to be incompatible with each other, either when both are true or false, or one is true and the other false (as in "this number is either even or odd"), or when their incompatibility is denied (as in "not, either this man is an animal or black"). 39

The First Section: On the Categorical Proposition

Containing four discussions

The First Discussion: On Its Parts and Divisions The categorical proposition is only realized through three parts: that on which judgment is passed (which is called the subject), that which is judged of it (which is called the predicate), and the relation between the two by which the predicate is connected to the subject; the expression signifying this relation is called a copula, like "is" in "Zayd is knowing." In this case, the proposition is called three-part. The copula may be omitted in some languages because the mind is aware of its meaning; in this case, the proposition is called two-part. 40

٤١ وهذه النسبة إن كانت نسبة يصحّ بها أن يقال إنّ الموضوع محمول فالقضيّة موجبة كقولنا الإنسان حيوان وإن كانت نسبة بها يصحّ أن يقال إنّ الموضوع ليس بمحمول فالقضيّة سالبة كقولنا الإنسان ليس بحجر.

٤٢ وموضوع الحمليّة إن كان شخصاً معيناً سمّيت القضيّة مخصوصة وشخصيّة وإن كان كليّاً فإن بُيّن فيها كمّيّة أفراد ما عليه الحكم ويسمّى اللفظ الدالّ عليها سوراً سمّيت محصورة ومسوّرة وهي أربع لأنّه إن بُيّن أنّ الحكم على كلّ الأفراد فهي الكلّيّة إمّا موجبة وسورها كلّ كقولنا كلّ نار حارّة وإمّا سالبة وسورها لا شيء ولا واحد كقولنا لا شيء ولا واحد من الإنسان بجماد وإن بُيّن فيها أنّ الحكم على بعض الأفراد فهي الجزئيّة إمّا موجبة وسورها بعض وواحد كقولنا بعض الحيوان إنسان وإمّا سالبة وسورها ليس كلّ وليس بعض وبعض ليس كقولنا ليس كلّ حيوان إنساناً.

٤٣ وإن لم يُبيّن فيها كمّيّة الأفراد فإن لم تصلح لأن تصدق كلّيّة وجزئيّة سمّيت القضيّة طبيعيّة كقولنا الحيوان جنس والإنسان نوع وإن صلحت لذلك سمّيت مهملة كقولنا الإنسان في خسر الإنسان ليس في خسر.

٤٤ وهي في قوّة الجزئيّة لأنّه متى صدق الإنسان في خسر صدق بعض الإنسان في خسر وبالعكس.

٤٥ البحث الثاني في تحقيق المحصورات الأربع قولنا كلّ ج ب يُستعمل تارة بحسب الحقيقة ومعناه أنّ كلّ ما لو وُجد كان[١] ج من الأفراد الممكنة فهو بحيث إذا وُجد كان ب أي كلّ ما هو ملزوم ج فهو ملزوم ب وتارة بحسب الخارج ومعناه كلّ ج في الخارج سواءً كان حال الحكم أو قبله أو بعده فهو ب في الخارج.

١ (لو وجد كان) في س، ف، ك؛ ت، ر: لو وجد وكان.

If the relation is such that it is correct to say that the subject has a given predicate, the proposition is affirmative, like "man is an animal." If the relation is such that it is correct to say that the subject does not have a given predicate, it is negative, like "man is not a stone." 41

If the subject of a categorical proposition is a specified individual, the proposition is called singular. If the subject is universal, and if the quantity of the individuals of which the judgment is true is made clear in the proposition (the expression signifying the quantity being called "quantifier"), then the proposition is called quantified. There are four kinds of quantified proposition. If it is made clear that the judgment is on all the individuals, the proposition is universal. The universal is either affirmative, its quantifier being "every" (as in "every fire is hot"), or negative, its quantifier being "no" or "not one" (as in "no man is inanimate"). If it is made clear in the proposition that the judgment is on some of the individuals, it is particular. The particular is either affirmative, its quantifier being "some" or "one" (as in "some animal is a man"), or it is negative, its quantifier being "not every" or "some are not" (as in "not every animal is a man"). 42

If the quantity of the individuals is not made clear in it, then—if it is not fit to be true as a universal or a particular—the proposition is called natural, like "animal is a genus" and "man is a species." On the other hand, if it is fit to be true as a universal or a particular it is called indefinite, as in "man is in loss" and "man is not in loss."[20] 43

Such a proposition has the force of a particular, for if "man is in loss" is true, "some man is in loss" is true, and vice versa. 44

The Second Discussion: On Verifying the Four Quantified Propositions "Every C is B" is used occasionally according to the essence, and its meaning is that every possible individual that, were it to exist, would be a C, would be a B under the same assumption (that is, that it were to exist); in other words, everything that is an implicant of C is an implicant of B. And occasionally it is used according to external existence, and its meaning is that every C in external existence, whether at the time of the judgment or before it or after it, is B in external existence. 45

٤٦ والفرق بين الاعتبارين ظاهر فإنّه لو لم يوجد شيء من المربّعات في الخارج لصحّ أن يقال كلّ مربّع شكل بالاعتبار الأوّل دون الثاني ولو لم يوجد في الخارج من الأشكال إلّا المربّع لصحّ أن يقال كلّ شكل مربّع بالاعتبار الثاني دون الأوّل.

٤٧ وعلى هذا فقس المحصورات الباقية.

٤٨ البحث الثالث في العدول والتحصيل حرف السلب إن كان جزءاً من الموضوع كقولنا اللاحيّ جماد أو من المحمول كقولنا الجماد لاعالم أو منهما جميعاً سميّت القضيّة معدولة موجبة كانت أوسالبة وإن لم يكن جزءاً لشيء منهما سميّت محصّلة إن كانت موجبة وبسيطة إن كانت سالبة.

٤٩ والاعتبار بإيجاب القضيّة وسلبها بالنسبة الثبوتيّة والسلبيّة لا بطرفي القضيّة فإنّ قولنا كلّ ما ليس بحيّ فهو لا عالم موجبة مع أنّ طرفيها عدميّان وقولنا لا شيء من المتحرّك بساكن سالبة مع أنّ طرفيها وجوديّان.

١،٥٠ والسالبة البسيطة أعمّ من الموجبة المعدولة المحمول لصدق السلب عند عدم الموضوع دون الإيجاب فإنّ الإيجاب لا يصحّ إلّا على موجود محقّق كما في الخارجيّة الموضوع أو مقدّر كما في الحقيقيّة الموضوع وأمّا إذا كان الموضوع موجوداً فإنّهما متلازمان.

٢،٥٠ والفرق بينهما في اللفظ أمّا في الثلاثيّة فالقضيّة موجبة إن قُدّمت الرابطة على حرف السلب وسالبة إن أُخّرت عنها وأمّا في الثنائيّة فبالنيّة أو بالاصطلاح على تخصيص لفظ غير أو لا بالإيجاب المعدول ولفظ ليس بالسلب البسيط أو بالعكس.

The distinction between the two considerations is obvious. Were there no squares in external existence, it would be true to say "every square is a figure" under the first consideration but not the second; and were there no figures in external existence other than squares, it would be correct to say "every figure is a square" under the second consideration but not the first. 46

On this basis, work out the remaining quantified propositions.[21] 47

The Third Discussion: On the Indefinite and the Determinate If the negative particle is part of the subject (as in "the not-living is inanimate") or of the predicate (as in "the inanimate is not-knowing"),[22] or of both, the proposition, whether affirmative or negative, is called metathetic. But if the negative particle is not part of either term, the proposition is called determinate if it is affirmative, and simple if it is negative. 48

The consideration with respect to whether a proposition is affirmative or negative goes to the affirming or negating relation, and not to its two extremes. "Every not-living is not-knowing" is an affirmative even though both extremes are privatives; "no moving is at rest" is a negative even though both extremes are positive. 49

The simple negative proposition is weaker than the affirmative with an indefinite predicate, because the negative is true given the nonexistence of the subject, but the affirmative is not. This is because affirmation is only correct for a subject verified to exist (as in propositions whose subject is under an externalist reading) or assumed to exist (as in propositions whose subject is under an essentialist reading). If the subject does exist, the simple negative and affirmative with indefinite predicate imply each other. 50.1

The distinction between the two is in expression. In the three-part proposition, the proposition is affirmative if the copula comes before the negative particle, and negative if it comes after it. In the two-part proposition, the distinction comes down to intention, or technical usage specifying "non" for metathetic affirmation, and "not" for simple negation, or the reverse. 50.2

٥١ البحث الرابع في القضايا الموجّهة[١] لا بدّ لنسبة المحمولات إلى الموضوعات من كيفيّة إيجابيّة كانت النسبة أو سلبيّة كالضرورة والدوام واللاضرورة واللادوام وتسمّى تلك الكيفيّة مادّة القضيّة واللفظ الدالّ عليها يسمّى جهة القضيّة.

١،٥٢ والقضايا الموجّهة التي جرت العادة بالبحث عنها وعن أحكامها ثلاثة عشر منها بسيطة وهي التي حقيقتها إيجاب فقط أو سلب فقط ومنها مركّبة وهي التي حقيقتها تتركّب من إيجاب وسلب والبسائط ستّ.

٢،٥٢ الأولى الضروريّة المطلقة وهي التي يُحكم فيها بضرورة ثبوت المحمول للموضوع أو سلبه عنه ما دام ذات الموضوع موجوداً كقولنا بالضرورة كلّ إنسان حيوان وبالضرورة لا شيء من الإنسان بحجر.

٣،٥٢ الثانية الدائمة المطلقة وهي التي يُحكم فيها بدوام ثبوت المحمول للموضوع أو سلبه عنه ما دام ذات الموضوع موجوداً ومثالها إيجاباً وسلباً ما مرّ.

٤،٥٢ الثالثة المشروطة العامّة وهي التي يُحكم فيها بضرورة ثبوت المحمول للموضوع أو سلبه عنه بشرط وصف الموضوع كقولنا بالضرورة كلّ كاتب متحرّك الأصابع ما دام كاتباً وبالضرورة لا شيء من الكاتب بساكن الأصابع ما دام كاتباً.

٥،٥٢ الرابعة العرفيّة العامّة وهي التي يُحكم فيها بدوام ثبوت المحمول للموضوع أو سلبه عنه بشرط وصف الموضوع ومثالها إيجاباً وسلباً ما مرّ.

٦،٥٢ الخامسة المطلقة العامّة وهي التي يُحكم فيها بثبوت المحمول للموضوع أو سلبه عنه بالفعل كقولنا بالإطلاق العامّ كلّ إنسان متنفّس وبالإطلاق العامّ لا شيء من الإنسان بمتنفّس.

٧،٥٢ السادسة الممكنة العامّة وهي التي يُحكم فيها بارتفاع الضرورة المطلقة عن الجانب المخالف كقولنا بالإمكان العامّ كلّ نار حارّة وبالإمكان العامّ لا شيء من الحارّ ببارد.

٥٣ أمّا المركّبات فسبع الأولى المشروطة الخاصّة وهي المشروطة العامّة مع قيد اللادوام بحسب الذات وهي إن كانت موجبة كقولنا بالضرورة كلّ كاتب متحرّك

---

١ (الموجّهة) في ر، ف، ك؛ ت، س: الموجبة.

The Fourth Discussion: On Modal Propositions Inevitably, the relation of a predicate to its subject, whether affirmative or negative, has a certain quality like necessity, perpetuity, nonnecessity, or non-perpetuity. This quality is called the matter of the proposition, and the expression signifying it is called the mode of the proposition. 51

The modal propositions that are customarily investigated (along with their valuations) come to thirteen. Some are simple (those the essence of which is only affirmation or negation), and some are compound (those the essence of which is made up of both an affirmation and a negation). There are six simple propositions.[23] 52.1

The first, the absolute necessary proposition, is that in which affirming or negating the predicate of the subject is judged to be necessary as long as the essence of the subject exists, as in "necessarily, every man is an animal" and "necessarily, no man is a stone." 52.2

The second, the absolute perpetual proposition, is that in which affirming or negating the predicate of the subject is judged to be perpetual as long as the essence of the subject exists. The affirmative and negative examples for the absolute necessary proposition apply here too. 52.3

The third, the general conditional proposition,[24] is that in which affirming or negating the predicate of the subject is judged to be necessary on condition the subject is under a description, as in "necessarily, everyone writing moves his fingers as long as he is writing," and "necessarily, no one writing keeps his fingers still as long as he is writing." 52.4

The fourth, the general conventional proposition, is that in which affirming or negating the predicate of the subject is judged to be perpetual on condition the subject is under a description. The affirmative and negative examples for the general conditional proposition apply here too. 52.5

The fifth, the general absolute proposition, is that in which affirming or negating the predicate of the subject is judged to be actual, as in "by general absoluteness, every man breathes" and "by general absoluteness, no man breathes." 52.6

The sixth, the general possible proposition, is that in which the opposing absolute necessity is judged to be removed, as in "by general possibility, every fire is hot" and "by general possibility, no fire is cold." 52.7

There are seven compound propositions: The first, the special conditional proposition, is the general conditional proposition with the restriction of non-perpetuity with respect to the essence. If it is affirmative (as in "necessarily, 53

الأصابع ما دام كاتباً لا دائماً فتركيبها من موجبة مشروطة عامّة وسالبة مطلقة عامّة وإن كانت سالبة كقولنا بالضرورة لا شيء من الكاتب بساكن الأصابع ما دام كاتباً لا دائماً فتركيبها من سالبة مشروطة عامّة وموجبة مطلقة عامّة.

٥٤ الثانية العرفيّة الخاصّة وهي العرفيّة العامّة مع قيد اللادوام بحسب الذات وهي إن كانت موجبة فتركيبها من موجبة عرفيّة عامّة وسالبة مطلقة عامّة وإن كانت سالبة فمن سالبة عرفيّة عامّة وموجبة مطلقة عامّة ومثالها إيجاباً وسلباً ما مرّ.

٥٥ الثالثة الوجوديّة اللاضروريّة وهي المطلقة العامّة مع قيد اللاضرورة بحسب الذات وهي إن كانت موجبة كقولنا كلّ إنسان ضاحك بالفعل لا بالضرورة فتركيبها من موجبة مطلقة عامّة وسالبة ممكنة عامّة وإن كانت سالبة كقولنا لا شيء من الإنسان بضاحك بالفعل لا بالضرورة فتركيبها من سالبة مطلقة عامّة وموجبة ممكنة عامّة.

٥٦ الرابعة الوجوديّة اللادائمة وهي المطلقة العامّة مع قيد اللادوام بحسب الذات وهي سواءً كانت موجبة أو سالبة فتركيبها من مطلقتين عامّتين إحداهما موجبة والأخرى سالبة ومثالها إيجاباً وسلباً ما مرّ.

٥٧ الخامسة الوقتيّة وهي التي يُحكم فيها بضرورة ثبوت المحمول للموضوع أو سلبه عنه في وقت معيّن من أوقات وجود الموضوع مقيّداً باللادوام بحسب الذات وهي إن كانت موجبة كقولنا بالضرورة كلّ قمر منخسف وقت حيلولة الأرض بينه وبين الشمس لا دائماً فتركيبها من موجبة وقتيّة مطلقة وسالبة مطلقة عامّة وإن كانت سالبة كقولنا بالضرورة لا شيء من القمر بمنخسف وقت التربيع لا دائماً فتركيبها من سالبة وقتيّة مطلقة وموجبة مطلقة عامّة.

٥٨ السادسة المنتشرة وهي التي يُحكم فيها بضرورة ثبوت المحمول للموضوع أو سلبه عنه في وقت غير معيّن من أوقات وجود الموضوع مقيّداً باللادوام بحسب الذات وهي إن كانت موجبة كقولنا بالضرورة كلّ إنسان متنفّس في وقت ما لا دائماً فتركيبها من موجبة منتشرة مطلقة وسالبة مطلقة عامّة وإن كانت سالبة كقولنا

everyone writing moves his fingers as long as he is writing, not always"), it is made up of an affirmative general conditional and a negative general absolute. If it is negative (as in "necessarily, no one writing keeps his fingers still as long as he is writing, not always"), it is made up of a negative general conditional and an affirmative general absolute.

The second, the special conventional proposition, is the general conventional proposition with the restriction of non-perpetuity with respect to the essence. If it is affirmative, it is made up of an affirmative general conventional and a negative general absolute; if it is negative, it is made up of a negative general conventional and an affirmative general absolute. The affirmative and negative examples for the special conditional proposition apply here too. 54

The third, the nonnecessary existential proposition, is the general absolute with the restriction of nonnecessity with respect to the essence. If it is affirmative (as in "every man actually laughs, not necessarily"), it is made up of an affirmative general absolute and a negative general possible. If it is negative (as in "no man actually laughs, not necessarily"), it is made up of a negative general absolute and an affirmative general possible. 55

The fourth, the non-perpetual existential proposition, is the general absolute with the restriction of non-perpetuity with respect to the essence. Whether affirmative or negative, it is made up of two general absolute propositions, one of which is affirmative and the other negative. The affirmative and negative examples for the nonnecessary existential proposition apply here too. 56

The fifth, the temporal, is that in which affirming or negating the predicate of the subject is judged to be necessary at one specified moment during the existence of the subject, with the restriction of non-perpetuity with respect to the essence. If it is affirmative (as in "necessarily, every moon is eclipsed on the earth's coming between it and the sun, not always"), it is made up of an affirmative absolute temporal and a negative general absolute. If it is negative (as in "necessarily, no moon is eclipsed at the moment of quadrature, not always"), it is made up of a negative absolute temporal and an affirmative general absolute. 57

The sixth, the spread proposition, is that in which affirming or negating the predicate of the subject is judged to be necessary at an unspecified moment during the existence of the subject, restricted by non-perpetuity with respect to the essence. If it is affirmative (as in "necessarily, every man breathes at a given time, not always"), it is made up of an affirmative absolute spread and a 58

بالضرورة لا شيء من الإنسان بمتنفّس وقتاً ما لا دائماً فتركيبها من سالبة منتشرة مطلقة وموجبة مطلقة عامّة.

١،٥٩ السابعة الممكنة الخاصّة وهي التي يُحكم فيها بارتفاع الضرورة المطلقة عن جانبي الوجود والعدم جميعاً وهي سواءً كانت موجبة كقولنا بالإمكان الخاصّ كلّ إنسان كاتب أو سالبة كقولنا بالإمكان الخاصّ لا شيء من الإنسان بكاتب فتركيبها من ممكنتين عامّتين إحداهما موجبة والأخرى سالبة.

٢،٥٩ والضابط أنّ اللادوام إشارة إلى مطلقة عامّة واللاضرورة إلى ممكنة عامّة متخالفتي الكيفيّة متوافقتي الكمّيّة للقضيّة المقيّدة بهما.

الفصل الثاني في أقسام الشرطيّة

١،٦٠ الجزء الأوّل منها يسمّى مقدّماً والثاني تالياً وهي إمّا متّصلة أو منفصلة.[١]

٢،٦٠ أمّا المتّصلة فإمّا لزوميّة وهي التي صدق التالي فيها على تقدير صدق المقدّم لعلاقة بينهما توجب ذلك كالعلّيّة والتضايف وإمّا اتّفاقيّة وهي التي يكون ذلك فيها لمجرّد توافق الجزئين على الصدق كقولنا إن كان الإنسان ناطقاً فالحمار ناهق.

٣،٦٠ وأمّا المنفصلة فإمّا حقيقيّة وهي التي يُحكم فيها بالتنافي بين جزئيها في الصدق والكذب معاً كقولنا إمّا أن يكون هذا العدد زوجاً أو فرداً وإمّا مانعة الجمع وهي التي يُحكم فيها بالتنافي بين الجزئين في الصدق فقط كقولنا إمّا أن يكون هذا الشيء حجراً أو شجراً وإمّا مانعة الخلوّ وهي التي يُحكم فيها بالتنافي بين الجزئين في الكذب فقط كقولنا إمّا أن يكون زيد في البحر أو لا يغرق.

٦١ وكلّ واحدة من هذه الثلاث إمّا عناديّة وهي التي يكون التنافي فيها لذاتي الجزئين كما في الأمثلة المذكورة وإمّا اتّفاقيّة وهي التي يكون التنافي فيها لمجرّد الاتّفاق كقولنا

١ (وهي إمّا متّصلة أو منفصلة) في ف؛ ساقطة من ت، ر، س، ك.

negative general absolute. If it is negative (as in "necessarily, no man is breathing at a given time, not always"), it is made up of a negative absolute spread and an affirmative general absolute.

The seventh, the special possible proposition, is that in which absolute necessity is judged to be removed, both as to the predicate's existence and its privation. Whether affirmative (as in "by special possibility, every man is a writer") or negative (as in "by special possibility, no man is a writer"), the special possible is made up of two general possible propositions, one affirmative and the other negative. 59.1

The guideline regarding these restrictions is that non-perpetuity points to a general absolute proposition, and nonnecessity to a general possible proposition, each disagreeing in quality but agreeing in quantity with the proposition it restricts. 59.2

The Second Section: On the Divisions of the Hypothetical Proposition

The first part of a hypothetical proposition is called antecedent and the second consequent. It is either conditional or disjunctive. 60.1

The conditional is either implicative or coincidental. In the implicative, the consequent is true on the supposition that the antecedent is true due to a connection between the two which necessitates that (as in causality or correlation). In the coincidental, the consequent is true by virtue of the two parts simply coinciding in being true (as in, "if man is rational, the donkey brays"). 60.2

The disjunctive is either exclusive, in which it is judged that the two parts are mutually incompatible with each other if true together or false together, as in "this number is either even or odd"; or alternative denial, in which it is judged that the two parts are incompatible with each other only when both are true, as in "this thing is either a stone or a tree"; or inclusive, in which it is judged that the two parts are incompatible with each other only when both are false, as in "either Zayd is in the water or else he will not be drowned." 60.3

Each of the three kinds of disjunction is either oppositional, in which the mutual exclusion is due to the two parts themselves, as in the examples above, or coincidental, in which the mutual exclusion just happens to be the case, as for example by positing someone who is black and not a writer, we have "this 61

للأسود اللاكاتب إمّا أن يكون أسود أو كاتباً حقيقيّة أو لا أسود أو كاتباً مانعة الجمع أو أسود أو لا كاتباً مانعة الخلوّ.

وسالبة كلّ واحدة من هذه القضايا الثمان هي التي ترفع ما حكم به[١] في موجبتها ٦٢ فسالبة اللزوم تسمّى سالبة لزوميّة وسالبة العناد تسمّى سالبة عناديّة وسالبة الاتّفاق تسمّى سالبة اتّفاقيّة.

والمتّصلة الموجبة تصدق عن صادقين وكاذبين وعن مجهولي الصدق والكذب ٦٣ وعن مقدّم كاذب وتال صادق دون عكسه لامتناع استلزام الصادق الكاذب وتكذب عن جزئين كاذبين وعن مقدّم كاذب وتال صادق وبالعكس وعن صادقين إذا كانت لزوميّة وأمّا إذا كانت اتّفاقيّة فكذبها عن صادقين محال.

المنفصلة الموجبة الحقيقيّة تصدق عن صادق وكاذب وتكذب عن صادقين ٦٤ وكاذبين والمانعة الجمع تصدق عن كاذبين وعن صادق وكاذب وتكذب عن صادقين والمانعة الخلوّ تصدق عن صادقين وعن صادق وكاذب وتكذب عن كاذبين والسالبة تصدق عمّا تكذب الموجبة وتكذب عمّا تصدق.

وكلّيّة الشرطيّة أن يكون التالي لازماً أو معانداً للمقدّم على جميع الأوضاع التي ١،٦٥ يمكن حصوله عليها وهي الأوضاع التي تحصل بسبب اقتران الأمور التي يمكن اجتماعه معها والجزئيّة أن تكون كذلك على بعض هذه الأوضاع والمخصوصة أن تكون كذلك على وضع معيّن.

وسور الموجبة الكلّيّة في المتّصلة كلّما ومهما ومتى وفي المنفصلة دائماً وسور ٢،٦٥ السالبة الكلّيّة فيهما ليس البتّة والموجبة الجزئيّة قد يكون والسالبة الجزئيّة قد لا يكون وبإدخال حرف السلب على سور الإيجاب الكلّيّ والمهملة بإطلاق لفظ لو وإن وإذا في المتّصلة وإمّا في المنفصلة.

والشرطيّة قد تتركّب عن حمليّتين وعن متّصلتين وعن منفصلتين وعن حمليّة ٦٦ ومتّصلة وعن حمليّة ومنفصلة وعن متّصلة ومنفصلة وكلّ واحدة من الثلاثة الأخيرة

---

١ (ما حكم به) في ف، ك؛ ت، س، ر: ما حكم.

person is either black or a writer" as an exclusive disjunction, or "not-black or a writer" as an alternative denial, or "black or a not-writer" as an inclusive.

The negative of each of these eight propositions is that which removes what 62
is judged to be in their affirmatives. So that which negates implication is called a negative implicative, that which negates opposition is called a negative oppositional, and that which negates what happens to be the case is called a negative coincidental.

The affirmative conditional may be true with two true and two false constitu- 63
ent propositions; and with two unknown as to truth and falsity; and with a false antecedent and true consequent (but not the reverse, because it is impossible that a true proposition entail a false one). The affirmative conditional may be false with two false parts; and with a false antecedent and true consequent, and the reverse; and with two true propositions (that is, if it is implicative; if it is coincidental, it is impossible for it to be false with two true propositions).

The affirmative exclusive disjunctive is true with one true and one false prop-
osition; it is false with two true and two false propositions. Alternative denial is 64
true with two false propositions, and with a true and a false; it is false with two true ones. The inclusive is true with two true propositions, and with a true one and a false one; it is false with two false ones. The negative is true of that of which the affirmative is false, and false of that of which the affirmative is true.

Universality for the hypothetical proposition is that the consequent be 65.1
implied by or opposed to the antecedent under all situations in which the antecedent can occur—that is to say, the situations that may arise for the antecedent by reason of being connected with matters that are compatible with it. It is the same for the particular hypothetical proposition under some of these situations; likewise for the singular under a specified situation.

The quantifiers for the universal affirmative in the conditional are "when- 65.2
ever," "whatever," and "when"; in the disjunctive, "always." The quantifier for the universal negative is "never" in both conditional and disjunctive. The quantifier for the particular affirmative is "sometimes" in both, and for the particular negative "sometimes not" in both (and also for the particular negative by inserting the negative particle in the quantifier for the universal affirmative). The quantifier for the indefinite in the conditional is by attaching "were it" and "if," and in the disjunctive, "either."[25]

The hypothetical may be made up of two categorical propositions, or two 66
conditionals, or two disjunctives, or a categorical and a conditional, or a

في المتّصلة تنقسم إلى قسمين لامتياز مقدّمها عن تاليها بالطبع بخلاف المنفصلة فإنّ مقدّمها إنّما يتميّز عن تاليها بالوضع فقط فأقسام المتّصلات تسعة والمنفصلات ستّة وأمّا الأمثلة فعليك باستخراجها من نفسك.

الفصل الثالث في أحكام القضايا
وفيه أربع مباحث

٦٧ البحث[١] الأوّل في التناقض حدّوه بأنّه اختلاف قضيّتين بالإيجاب والسلب بحيث يقتضي لذاته أن تكون إحداهما صادقة والأخرى كاذبة.

٦٨ ولا يتحقّق في المخصوصتين إلّا عند اتّحاد الموضوع وتندرج فيه وحدة الشرط والجزء والكلّ وعند اتّحاد المحمول وتندرج فيه وحدة الزمان والمكان والإضافة والقوّة والفعل وفي المحصورتين لا بدّ مع ذلك من الاختلاف بالكمّيّة لصدق الجزئيّتين وكذب الكلّيّتين في كلّ مادّة يكون الموضوع فيها أعمّ ولا بدّ من الاختلاف في الكلّ بالجهة لصدق الممكنتين وكذب الضروريّتين في مادّة الإمكان.

١،٦٩ فنقيض الضروريّة المطلقة الممكنة العامّة لأنّ سلب الضرورة مع الضرورة ممّا يتناقضان جزماً.

٢،٦٩ ونقيض الدائمة المطلقة العامّة لأنّ السلب في كلّ الأوقات يناقضه الإثبات في البعض[٢] وبالعكس.

٣،٦٩ ونقيض المشروطة العامّة الحينيّة الممكنة أعني التي حُكم فيها برفع الضرورة بحسب الوصف عن الجانب المخالف كقولنا كلّ من به ذات الجنب يمكن أن يسعل في بعض أوقات كونه مجنوباً.

---

١ (البحث) في س، ف، ك؛ ساقطة من ت، ر. ٢ (في البعض) في س، ف، ك؛ ت، ر: في بعضه.

categorical and a disjunctive, or a conditional and a disjunctive. Each of the last three divides, if conditional, into two subdivisions, due to the distinction by nature between their antecedent and consequent. This is in contrast to the disjunctive, for its antecedent is distinguished from the consequent only by its placement. So there are nine divisions of conditionals, and six of disjunctives. You should extract their forms for yourself.

The Third Section: On the Valuations of Propositions

Containing four discussions

The First Discussion: On Contradiction Contradiction has been defined as a difference between two propositions in affirmation and negation such that it requires of itself that one is true and the other false. 67

The contradiction of two singular propositions is only realized when the subjects of both propositions are the same (under which must be considered unity of condition, and of part and whole), and if the predicates in both propositions are the same (under which must be considered unity of time, place, relation, potentiality, and actuality). With respect to two quantified propositions, there must be, in addition to the above, a difference in quantity (because the two particulars are true and the two universals are false in every propositional matter in which the subject is more general than the predicate). In all propositions, there must also be a difference in modality (because the two possible propositions are true and the two necessary propositions are false in contingent matter). 68

The contradictory of the absolute necessary proposition is the general possible proposition, because the negation of necessity and necessity are certainly mutually contradictory. 69.1

The contradictory of the absolute perpetual proposition is the general absolute, because negation at every moment contradicts affirmation at some moment, and vice versa. 69.2

The contradictory of the general conditional is the possible continuing: I mean, that in which it is judged to remove the opposing necessity with respect to the description, as in “everyone afflicted with pleurisy may cough at times while afflicted.” 69.3

٤،٦٩ ونقيض العرفيّة العامّة الحينيّة المطلقة أعني التي حُكم فيها بثبوت المحمول للموضوع أو سلبه عنه في بعض أحيان وصف الموضوع ومثالها ما مرّ.

٧٠ وأمّا المركّبات فإن كانت كلّيّة فنقيضها أحد نقيضي جزئيها وذلك جليّ بعد الإحاطة بحقائق المركّبات ونقائض البسائط فإنّك إذا تحقّقت أنّ الوجوديّة اللادائمة تركيبها من مطلقتين عامّتين إحداهما موجبة والأخرى سالبة وأنّ نقيض المطلقة هو الدائمة تحقّقت أنّ نقيضها إمّا الدائم المخالف أو الدائم الموافق.

٧١ وإن كانت جزئيّة فلا يكفي في نقيضها ما ذكرناه لأنّه يكذب بعض الجسم حيوان لا دائماً مع كذب كلّ واحد من نقيضي جزئيها بل الحقّ في نقيضها أن يردَّد بين نقيضي الجزئين لكلّ واحد واحد أي كلّ واحد واحد لا يخلو عن نقيضيهما[١] فيقال كلّ جسم إمّا حيوان دائماً أو ليس بحيوان دائماً.

٧٢ وأمّا الشرطيّة فنقيض الكلّيّة منها الجزئيّة الموافقة في الجنس والنوع المخالفة في الكيف والكم وبالعكس.[٢]

٧٣ البحث الثاني في العكس المستوي وهو عبارة عن جعل الجزء الأوّل من القضيّة ثانياً والثاني أوّلاً مع بقاء الصدق والكيفيّة.

٧٤ أمّا السوالب فإن كانت كلّيّة فسبع منها وهي الوقتيّتان والوجوديّتان والممكنتان والمطلقة العامّة لا تنعكس لامتناع العكس في أخصّها وهي الوقتيّة لصدق قولنا بالضرورة لا شيء من القمر بمنخسف وقت التربيع لا دائماً وكذب بعض المنخسف ليس بقمر بالإمكان العامّ الذي هو أعمّ الجهات لأنّ كلّ منخسف فهو قمر بالضرورة وإذا

---

١ (نقيضيهما) في ف؛ ت، ر، س، ك: نقيضها. ٢ (الموافقة في الجنس والنوع المخالفة في الكيف والكم وبالعكس) في ك؛ ت، ر: الموافقة في الجنس المخالفة في الكيفية وبالعكس.

The contradictory of the general conventional is the absolute continuing: I mean, that in which it is judged to affirm or negate the predicate of the subject at some of the moments the description of the subject holds; the preceding example serves here too.[26] 69.4

70 Let us turn to compound propositions. If the compound is universal, its contradictory is one of the contradictories of its two parts. This is clear once you have understood the realities of compound propositions and the contradictories of simple propositions. So, if you have verified that the non-perpetual existential is made up of two general absolute propositions, one of which is affirmative and the other negative, and that the contradictory of the absolute is the perpetual proposition, then you have also verified that the contradictory of the compound is either the perpetual proposition that opposes the original in quantity and quality, or the perpetual proposition that agrees with the original.[27]

71 If the compound proposition is particular, however, what we have mentioned will not be sufficient to find a contradictory for it, for "some bodies are animals, not always" is false, and so are both of the contradictories of its two parts. The truth in forming the contradictory is to flank a disjunctive with the contradictories of the two parts for every one of the subjects—that is, each taken one by one must have both contradictories, so "every body is either always an animal or always not an animal."

72 The contradictory of the universal hypothetical is the particular that agrees with it in genus and species, but that opposes it in quality and quantity, and vice versa.[28]

73 *The Second Discussion: On Straight Conversion* Straight conversion consists of placing the first part of a proposition second and the second part first, with the truth and quality remaining in the converse as they were in the convertend.[29]

74 Consider the negatives: If the negative is universal, there are seven modalities that cannot be converted—namely, the two temporals, the two existentials, the two possibles, and the general absolute. This is because of the impossibility of converting the strongest of them, the temporal, due to the truth of "necessarily, no moon is eclipsed at the time of quadrature, not always," and the falsity of "some of what is eclipsed is not a moon" by general possibility (which is the weakest of the modalities), because everything that is eclipsed is necessarily a moon. If the strongest does not convert, neither does the weaker;

لم ينعكس الأخصّ لم ينعكس الأعمّ إذ لو انعكس الأعمّ لانعكس الأخصّ لأنّ لازم الأعمّ لازم الأخصّ ضرورة.

٧٥ وأمّا الضروريّة والدائمة المطلقتان فتنعكسان دائمة كلّيّة لأنّه إذا صدق بالضرورة أو دائماً لا شيء من ج ب فدائماً لا شيء من ب ج وإلّا فبعض ب ج بالإطلاق العامّ وهو مع الأصل ينتج بعض ب ليس ب بالضرورة في الضروريّة ودائماً في الدائمة وهو محال.

١،٧٦ وأمّا المشروطة والعرفيّة العامّتان فتنعكسان عرفيّة عامّة كلّيّة لأنّه إذا صدق بالضرورة أو دائماً لا شيء من ج ب ما دام ج فدائماً لا شيء من ب ج ما دام ب وإلّا فبعض ب ج حين هو ب وهو مع الأصل ينتج بعض ب ليس ب حين هو ب وهو محال.

٢،٧٦ وأمّا المشروطة والعرفيّة الخاصّتان فتنعكسان عرفيّة عامّة لا دائمة في البعض[1] أمّا العرفيّة العامّة فلكونها لازمة للعامّتين وأمّا اللادوام فلأنّه لو كذب لصدق لا شيء من ب ج دائماً فتنعكس لا شيء من ج ب دائماً وقد كان كلّ ج ب بالفعل هذا خلف.

١،٧٧ وإن كانت جزئيّة فالمشروطة والعرفيّة الخاصّتان تنعكسان عرفيّة خاصّة لأنّه إذا صدق بالضرورة أو دائماً بعض ج ليس ب ما دام ج لا دائماً وجب أن يصدق بعض ب ليس ج ما دام ب لا دائماً لأنّا نفرض ذات الموضوع وهو ج د فد ج بالفعل ود ب أيضاً للادوام سلب الباء عنه وليس ج ما دام ب وإلّا لكان ج حين هو ب فب حين هو ج وقد كان ليس ب ما دام ج هذا خلف وإذا صدق الباء والجيم عليه وتنافيا فيه صدق بعض ب ليس ج ما دام ب لا دائماً وهو المطلوب.

٢،٧٧ وأمّا البواقي فلا تنعكس لأنّه يصدق بالضرورة بعض الحيوان ليس بإنسان وبالضرورة بعض القمر ليس بمنخسف وقت التربيع لا دائماً مع كذب عكسهما بالإمكان العامّ لكنّ الضروريّة أخصّ البسائط والوقتيّة أخصّ المركّبات الباقية

١ (في البعض) في س، ف، ك؛ ت، ر: للبعض.

for were the weaker to convert, so would the stronger (because the implicate of the weaker is necessarily the implicate of the stronger).[30]

The absolute necessary and absolute perpetual propositions convert as a universal perpetual, because if it is of necessity, or always, true that "no C is B," then always "no B is C"; were it not the case, then "some B is C" as a general absolute proposition, and this, together with the original proposition, would produce "some B is not B by necessity" for the necessary proposition, and "some B is not B always" for the perpetual proposition; this is absurd. 75

The general conditional and the general conventional convert as a universal general conventional, because if it is of necessity, or always, true that "no C is B as long as it is C," then "always, no B is C as long as it is B"; were it not the case, then "some B is C while B," and this with the original proposition produces "some B is not B while B"; this is absurd. 76.1

The special conditional and special conventional convert as a general conventional, which is non-perpetual-for-some. The general conventional component of the converse follows because it is the implicate of both the general conditional and conventional propositions; the component that is non-perpetual-for-some follows because, were it false, "always, no B is C" would be true, which converts as "always, no C is B"; but it was the case that every C is B actually. This is absurd. 76.2

Turning to the particulars: Both the special conditional and conventional convert as a special conventional, because if it is of necessity, or always, true that "some C is not B as long as it is C, not always," then "some B is not C as long as it is B, not always" must be true, because we may expose what underlies the subject, C, as D; then D is C actually, and D is also B due to the non-perpetual rider relative to negating B of C; further, D is not C as long as it is B (otherwise, D would be C while B, and so B while C; yet it was the case C is not B as long as it is C; this is absurd). And if B and C are true of D and are incompatible with each other, it is true that "some B is not C as long as it is B, not always," which is what is sought. 77.1

The remaining particular propositions do not convert. This is because "necessarily, some animals are not human" and "necessarily, some moon is not eclipsed at the time of quadrature, not always" are true, while their converses as general possible propositions are false. But the necessary proposition is the strongest of the simple propositions, and the temporal the strongest of the remaining compound propositions. When they do not convert, neither does 77.2

ومتى لم تنعكسا لم ينعكس شيء منها لما عرفت أنّ انعكاس العامّ مستلزم لانعكاس الخاصّ.

١،٧٨ وأمّا الموجبة فكلّيّة كانت أو جزئيّة فلا تنعكس كلّيّة لاحتمال كون المحمول أعمّ وأمّا في الجهة فالضروريّة والدائمة والعامّتان تنعكس حينيّة مطلقة لأنّه إذا صدق كلّ ج ب بإحدى الجهات الأربع المذكورة فبعض ب ج حين هو ب وإلّا فلا شيء من ب ج ما دام ب وهو مع الأصل ينتج لا شيء من ج ج دائماً في الضروريّة والدائمة وما دام ج في العامّتين وهو محال.

٢،٧٨ وأمّا الخاصّتان فتنعكسان حينيّة مطلقة مقيّدة باللادوام أمّا الحينيّة المطلقة فلكونها لازمة لعامّتيهما وأمّا قيد اللادوام في الأصل الكلّيّ فلأنّه لو كذب لصدق كلّ ب ج دائماً فنضمّه إلى الجزء الأوّل من الأصل وهو قولنا بالضرورة أو دائماً كلّ ج ب ما دام ج ينتج كلّ ب ب دائماً ونضمّه إلى الجزء الثاني أيضاً وهو قولنا لا شيء من ج ب بالإطلاق العامّ فينتج لا شيء من ب ب بالإطلاق العامّ فيلزم اجتماع النقيضين وهو محال.

٣،٧٨ وأمّا في الجزئي فتفرض الموضوع د فهو لا ج بالفعل وإلّا لكان ج دائماً ف ب دائماً لدوام الباء بدوام الجيم لكنّ اللازم باطل لتقيّد[1] الأصل باللادوام.

٤،٧٨ وأمّا الوقتيّتان والوجوديّتان والمطلقة العامّة فتنعكس مطلقة عامّة لأنّه إذا صدق كلّ ج ب بإحدى الجهات الخمس المذكورة فبعض ب ج بالإطلاق العامّ وإلّا فلا شيء من ب ج دائماً وهو مع الأصل ينتج لا شيء من ج ج دائماً وهو محال.

٧٩ وإن شئت عكست نقيض العكس في الموجبات ليصدق نقيض الأصل أو الأخصّ منه.

٨٠ وأمّا الممكنتان فحالهما في الانعكاس وعدمه غير معلوم لتوقّف البرهان المذكور للانعكاس فيهما على انعكاس السالبة الضروريّة كنفسها وعلى إنتاج الصغرى الممكنة

١ (لتقيّد) في ر، س، ك؛ ت :لقيد.

any other proposition, due to what you have learned: the conversion of the weak entails the conversion of the strong.

The affirmative, whether universal or particular, does not convert as a universal due to the possibility that the predicate is more general than the subject. Turning to modality, the necessary, the perpetual, the general conditional, and the general conventional convert as an absolute continuing. This is because if "every C is B" is true under any of the four modalities mentioned, "some B is C while B." Were this not the case, then "always, no B is C as long as it is B," which, with the original proposition, produces "always, no C is C" in the case of the necessary and the perpetual, and "always, no C is C as long as it is C" in the case of the two generals; these conclusions are absurd. 78.1

The two specials convert as absolute continuing restricted by non-perpetuity. The absolute continuing component is due to its being an implicate of the two generals. The non-perpetuity rider from the original universal proposition is there because, were it false that some B is not C actually, it would be true "always, every B is C"; we add this to the first part of the original proposition ("necessarily or always, every C is B as long as it is C"), which produces "always, every B is B." Now add it also to the second part ("no C is B" by a general absoluteness), which produces "no B is B" by a general absoluteness; so it follows that two contradictories are conjoined, and this is absurd. 78.2

To convert the particular of the special conditional and special conventional, expose from the subject C D such that it is actually not C, otherwise it would always be C, and thus always B due to B's perpetuity as a function of the perpetuity of C. But the implicate is false due to the restriction of the original proposition by non-perpetuity. 78.3

The two temporals, the two existentials, and the general absolute convert as a general absolute. This is because if "every C is B" is true under one of the five modalities mentioned, then "some B is C" by general absoluteness. Were this not the case, then "always, no B is C" would be true and, with the original proposition, produces "always, no C is C"; this is absurd. 78.4

If you wish, you may when dealing with affirmative propositions convert the contradictory of the converse so that the contradictory of the original proposition (or what is stronger than it) would be true. 79

The status of the two possible propositions with respect to conversion or its failure is unknown due to the fact that the demonstration mentioned to prove their conversion depends on the conversion of the negative necessary 80

مع الكبرى الضروريّة في الشكل الأوّل اللذين كلّ منهما غير محقق ولعدم الظفر بدليل يوجب الانعكاس وعدمه.

٨١ وأمّا الشرطيّة فالمتّصلة الموجبة تنعكس موجبة جزئيّة والسالبة الكلّيّة سالبة كلّيّة إذ لو صدق نقيض العكس لانتظم مع الأصل قياساً منتجاً للمحال وأمّا السالبة الجزئيّة فلا تنعكس لصدق قولنا قد لا يكون إذا كان هذا حيواناً فهو إنسان مع كذب العكس وأمّا المنفصلة فلا يُتصوّر فيها العكس لعدم الامتياز بين جزئيها بالطبع.

٨٢ البحث الثالث في عكس النقيض وهو عبارة عن جعل الجزء الأوّل من القضيّة نقيض الثاني والثاني عين الأوّل مع مخالفته الأصل في الكيف وموافقته في الصدق.

١،٨٣ وأمّا الموجبات فإن كانت كلّيّة فسبع منها وهي التي لا تنعكس سوالبها بالعكس المستوي لا تنعكس لأنّه يصدق بالضرورة كلّ قمر فهو ليس بمنخسف وقت التربيع لا دائماً دون عكسه لما عرفت.

٢،٨٣ وتنعكس الضروريّة والدائمة دائمة كلّيّة لأنّه إذا صدق بالضرورة أو دائماً كلّ ج ب فدائماً لا شيء ممّا ليس ب ج وإلّا فبعض ما ليس ب فهو ج بالفعل وهو مع الأصل ينتج بعض ما ليس ب فهو ب بالضرورة في الضروريّة ودائماً في الدائمة وهو محال.

٣،٨٣ وأمّا المشروطة والعرفيّة العامّتان فتنعكسان عرفيّة عامّة كلّيّة لأنّه إذا صدق بالضرورة أو دائماً كلّ ج ب ما دام ج فدائماً لا شيء ممّا ليس ب ج ما دام ليس ب وإلّا فبعض ما ليس ب فهو ج حين هو ليس ب وهو مع الأصل ينتج بعض ما ليس ب فهو ب حين هو ليس ب وهو محال.

٤،٨٣ وأمّا الخاصّتان فتنعكسان عرفيّة عامّة لا دائمة في البعض أمّا العرفيّة العامّة فلاستلزام العامّتين إيّاها وأمّا قيد اللادوام في البعض فلأنّه يصدق بعض ما ليس

proposition as itself, and on the productivity of a possible minor with a necessary major in the first figure, and neither of these can be verified. This in turn is due to lack of success in finding a proof that requires either that the possible converts or that it does not.

Affirmative conditional hypothetical propositions convert as particular affirmative, and the universal negative as universal negative; since were the contradictory of the converse true, it could be ordered with the original as a syllogism producing the absurd. The particular negative does not convert because "sometimes not, if this is an animal then this is a man" is true while the converse is false. Conversion in the disjunctive is inconceivable due to the lack of distinction between the two parts by nature. 81

The Third Discussion: On Contraposition Contraposition consists of making the contradictory of the second part of the original proposition the first part of the derived proposition, and leaving the first part of the original unchanged as the second part of the derived proposition; the derived proposition differs from the original in quality but agrees with it in truth.[31] 82

Consider universal affirmative propositions. Seven of them do not contrapose—namely, those whose negatives do not convert by straight conversion. This is because "necessarily, every moon is not-eclipsed at the time of quadrature, not always" is true while its contrapositive is not, due to what you have learned.[32] 83.1

The necessary proposition and the perpetual contrapose as perpetual universals because, if "necessarily, or always, every C is B" is true, then "always, nothing that is not-B is C." Were that not the case, then "some of what is not-B is C actually," and this with the original proposition produces "necessarily, some of what is not-B is B" (in the necessary proposition), or "always . . ." (in the perpetual proposition); this is absurd. 83.2

General conditional and conventional propositions contrapose as general conventional universals because, if "necessarily, or always, every C is B as long as it is C" is true, then "always, nothing that is not-B is C as long as it is not-B." Were that not so, then "some of what is not-B is C while not-B"; this with the original proposition produces "some of what is not-B is B while not-B," and this is absurd. 83.3

The special conditional and conventional propositions contrapose as general conventional non-perpetual-for-some. The general conventional part of 83.4

ب فهو ج بالإطلاق العامّ وإلّا فلا شيء ممّا ليس ب ج دائمًا فتنعكس لا شيء من ج ليس ب دائمًا وقد كان لا شيء من ج ب بالفعل بحكم اللادوام ويلزمه كلّ ج فهو ليس ب بالفعل لوجود الموضوع هذا خلف.

١،٨٤ وإن كانت جزئيّة فالخاصّتان تنعكسان عرفيّة خاصّة لأنّه إذا صدق بالضرورة أو دائمًا بعض ج ب ما دام ج لا دائمًا نفرض الموضوع وهو ج د فد ليس ب بالفعل للادوام ثبوت الباء له وليس ج ما دام ليس ب وإلّا لكان ج حين هو ليس ب فليس ب حين هو ج وقد كان ب ما دام ج هذا خلف ود ج بالفعل وهو ظاهر فبعض ما ليس ب ليس هو ج ما دام ليس ب لا دائمًا وهو المطلوب.

٢،٨٤ وأمّا البواقي فلا تنعكس لصدق قولنا بعض الحيوان هو ليس بإنسان بالضرورة المطلقة وبعض القمر هو ليس بمنخسف بالضرورة الوقتيّة دون عكسهما ومتى لم تنعكسا لم ينعكس شيء منها لما عرفت في العكس المستوي.

١،٨٥ وأمّا السوالب كلّيّة كانت أو جزئيّة فلا تنعكس كلّيّة لاحتمال أن يكون نقيض المحمول أعمّ من الموضوع وتنعكس الخاصّتان حينيّة مطلقة لأنّه إذا صدق بالضرورة أو دائمًا لا شيء من ج ب ما دام ج لا دائمًا نفرض الموضوع د فهو ليس ب بالفعل ود ج في بعض أوقات ليس ب لأنّه ليس ب في جميع أوقات ج فبعض ما ليس ب فهو ج في بعض أحيان ليس ب وهو المدّعى.

٢،٨٥ وأمّا الوقتيّتان والوجوديّتان فتنعكس[1] مطلقة عامّة لأنّه إذا صدق لا شيء من ج ب بإحدى هذه الجهات نفرض الموضوع د فهو ليس ب بالفعل ود ج فبعض ما ليس ب فهو ج بالفعل وهو المطلوب وهكذا تبيّن عكوس جزئيّاتها.

٨٦ وأمّا بواقي السوالب والشرطيّات موجبة كانت أو سالبة فغير معلومة الانعكاس لعدم الظفر بالبرهان.

---

١ (فتنعكس) في ر، س، ف، ك؛ ت :تنعكسان.

the contrapositive follows because both general propositions entail it. The non-perpetual-for-some part follows because "some of what is not-B is C" is true as a general absolute, otherwise "always, no not-B is C," which converts as "always, no C is not-B"; yet it is the case that "no C is B actually" (as a result of the judgment of non-perpetuity), from which it follows that "every C is not-B actually" (due to the existence of the subject in the original proposition); this is absurd.

If the original proposition is particular, then both the special conditional 84.1
and the special conventional contrapose as a special conventional. This is because if "necessarily, or always, some C is B as long as it is C, not always" is true, then let us expose part of the subject C as D; D is not-B actually due to the non-perpetuity of the affirmation of B of it, and is not C as long as it is not-B (otherwise it would be C while not-B, whereupon D would be not-B while it is C, yet it is B as long as it is C; this is absurd), and D is C actually; this is obvious. So "some of what is not-B is not C as long as it is not-B, not always," which is what is sought.

As for the rest, they do not contrapose. This is because "some animal is not- 84.2
man" is true by absolute necessity, and "some moon is not-eclipsed" is true by temporal necessity, yet their contrapositives are not true; since these two do not contrapose, nor do any of the weaker modals, due to what you learned in the treatment of straight conversion.

Negatives, whether universal or particular, do not contrapose as universal 85.1
due to the possibility that the contradictory of the predicate is more general than the subject. The two specials contrapose as absolute continuing because, if "necessarily, or always, no C is B as long as it is C, not always" is true, then let us expose part of the subject as D; D is not-B actually, and C at some times of its being not-B (because it is not-B at all times of its being C); so "some of what is not-B is C at some moments it is not-B." And that is what is claimed.

The two temporals and the two existentials all contrapose as a general abso- 85.2
lute. This is because if "no C is B" is true by one of these modalities, we expose part of the subject as D. So D is not-B actually, and C actually; so "some of what is not-B is C actually," which is what is sought. So too we may prove the contrapositives of the particulars.

As for the rest of the negatives, and the affirmative and negative hypotheti- 86
cal propositions: their status with respect to contraposition is unknown, due to lack of success in finding a proof.

١،٨٧ البحث الرابع في لوازم الشرطيّات أمّا المتّصلة الموجبة الكلّيّة فتستلزم منفصلة مانعة الجمع من عين المقدّم ونقيض التالي ومانعة الخلوّ من نقيض المقدّم وعين التالي متعاكسين عليها وإلّا لبطل اللزوم والانفصال.

٢،٨٧ وأمّا المنفصلة الحقيقيّة فتستلزم أربع متّصلات مقدّم اثنين عين أحد الجزئين وتاليهما نقيض الآخر ومقدّم الآخرين[١] نقيض أحد الجزئين وتاليهما عين الآخر.

٣،٨٧ وكلّ واحدة من غير الحقيقيّة مستلزمة للأخرى مركّبة من نقيضي الجزئين.

١ (مقدّم الآخرين) في ف، ك؛ ت، ر: آخرين.

The Fourth Discussion: On the Implicates of Hypothetical Propositions The affirmative universal conditional entails an alternative denial consisting of the original antecedent and the contradictory of the consequent, and an inclusive disjunctive consisting of the contradictory of the antecedent and the original consequent. And they both convert back to the original conditional, otherwise implication and disjunction mean nothing. 87.1

The exclusive disjunctive entails four conditional propositions. The antecedent of two of them is one of the two parts of the original proposition unchanged, each with a consequent that is the contradictory of the other part. The antecedent of the other two conditionals is the contradictory of one of the two parts, each with a consequent that is the other part unchanged. 87.2

Each of the other two nonexclusive disjunctives entails the other compounded of the contradictories of the two parts of the original proposition.[33] 87.3

المقالة الثالثة في القياس

وفيها خمسة فصول

الفصل الأوّل في تعريف القياس وأقسامه

٨٨ القياس قول مؤلّف من قضايا إذا سُلّمت لزم عنها لذاتها قول آخر.

١،٨٩ وهو استثنائيّ إن كان عين النتيجة أو نقيضها مذكورًا فيه بالفعل كقولنا إن كان هذا جسمًا فهو متحرّك لكنّه جسم أنتج أنّه متحرّك وهو بعينه مذكور فيه ولو قلنا لكنّه ليس بمتحرّك أنتج أنّه ليس بجسم ونقيضه مذكور فيه.

٢،٨٩ واقترانيّ إن لم يكن كذلك كقولنا كلّ جسم مؤلّف وكلّ مؤلّف حادث ينتج كلّ جسم حادث وليس هو ولا نقيضه مذكورًا فيه.

٩٠ وموضوع المطلوب فيه يسمّى أصغر ومحموله أكبر والقضيّة التي جُعلت جزء قياس تسمّى مقدّمة والمقدّمة التي فيها الأصغر الصغرى والتي فيها الأكبر الكبرى والمتكرّر بينهما حدًّا أوسط واقتران الصغرى والكبرى يسمّى قرينة وضربًا والهيئة الحاصلة من كيفيّة وضع الحدّ الأوسط عند الحدّين الآخرين تسمّى شكلًا وهو أربعة لأنّ الأوسط[1] إن كان محمولًا في الصغرى موضوعًا في الكبرى فهو الشكل الأوّل وإن كان محمولًا فيهما فهو الشكل الثاني وإن كان موضوعًا فيهما فهو الشكل الثالث وإن كان موضوعًا في الصغرى محمولًا في الكبرى فهو الشكل الرابع.

---

١ (الأوسط) في ك؛ ت، ر: الوسط.

The Third Treatise: On Syllogism

Containing five sections

The First Section: On Definition and Division of Syllogism

Syllogism is a discourse composed of propositions from which alone, if admitted, another discourse follows necessarily. 88

A syllogism is repetitive if the conclusion itself or its contradictory is actually mentioned in the syllogism, as in "if this is a body, it is mobile; but it is a body," which produces "it is mobile"; so the conclusion itself is mentioned in the syllogism. Were we to say "but it is not mobile," it would produce "it is not a body," the contradictory of which is actually mentioned in the syllogism. 89.1

If that is not the case, then the syllogism is connective, as in "every body is composite" and "every composite is produced in time," which produces "every body is produced in time"; neither the conclusion nor its contradictory is mentioned in the syllogism. 89.2

The subject of what is sought is called the minor term, and its predicate is called the major term. A proposition that is made part of a syllogism is called a premise. The premise that contains the minor term is called the minor premise, and the one that contains the major term is called the major premise. The term repeated in both is called the middle term. The connection between the minor and major premises is called the connection-form, or mood. The form resulting from how the middle term is positioned relative to the other two terms is called a figure. There are four figures, because if the middle term is predicate in the minor premise and subject in the major, it is first figure; if it is predicate in both, it is second figure; if it is subject in both, it is third figure; and if it is subject in the minor premise and predicate in the major, it is fourth figure. 90

أمّا الشكل الأوّل فشرطه إيجاب الصغرى وإلّا لم يندرج الأصغر في الأوسط وكلّيّة الكبرى وإلّا احتمل أن يكون البعض المحكوم عليه بالأكبر غير البعض المحكوم به على الأصغر وضروبه الناتجة أربعة. ١،٩١

الأوّل من موجبتين كلّيّتين ينتج موجبة كلّيّة كقولنا كلّ ج ب وكلّ ب ا فكلّ ج ا. ٢،٩١

الثاني من كلّيّتين والصغرى موجبة والكبرى سالبة ينتج سالبة كلّيّة كقولنا كلّ ج ب ولا شيء من ب ا ينتج لا شيء من ج ا. ٣،٩١

الثالث من موجبتين والصغرى جزئيّة ينتج موجبة جزئيّة كقولنا بعض ج ب وكلّ ب ا فبعض ج ا. ٤،٩١

الرابع من موجبة جزئيّة صغرى وسالبة كلّيّة كبرى ينتج سالبة جزئيّة كقولنا بعض ج ب ولا شيء من ب ا فبعض ج ليس ا. ٥،٩١

ونتائج هذا الشكل بيّنة بذاتها. ٦،٩١

أمّا الشكل الثاني فشرطه اختلاف مقدّمتيه بالكيف وكلّيّة الكبرى وإلّا لحصل الاختلاف الموجب لعدم الإنتاج وهو صدق القياس مع إيجاب النتيجة تارة ومع سلبها أخرى. ٩٢

وضروبه الناتجة أيضاً أربعة. ١،٩٣

الأوّل من كلّيّتين والصغرى موجبة ينتج سالبة كلّيّة كقولنا كلّ ج ب ولا شيء من ا ب فلا شيء من ج ا بالخلف وهو ضمّ نقيض النتيجة إلى الكبرى لينتج نقيض الصغرى وبانعكاس الكبرى ليرتدّ إلى الأوّل. ٢،٩٣

الثاني من كلّيّتين والكبرى موجبة ينتج سالبة كلّيّة كقولنا لا شيء من ج ب وكلّ ا ب فلا شيء من ج ا بالخلف وبعكس الصغرى وجعلها كبرى ثمّ عكس النتيجة. ٣،٩٣

الثالث من موجبة جزئيّة صغرى وسالبة كلّيّة كبرى ينتج سالبة جزئيّة كقولنا بعض ج ب ولا شيء من ا ب فليس بعض ج ا بالخلف وبعكس الكبرى ليرجع إلى ٤،٩٣

The conditions of productivity in the first figure are that the minor premise be affirmative (otherwise the minor term does not come under the middle term), and that the major premise be universal (otherwise it may be that the part of the middle of which the major term is predicated is not the part of the middle predicated of the minor term). This figure has four productive moods. 91.1

The first, with two universal affirmatives, produces a universal affirmative, as in "every C is B, every B is A, therefore every C is A." 91.2

The second, with two universals, the minor premise affirmative and the major negative, produces a universal negative, as in "every C is B, no B is A, therefore no C is A." 91.3

The third, with two affirmatives, the minor premise being a particular, produces a particular affirmative conclusion, as in "some C is B, every B is A, therefore some C is A." 91.4

The fourth, with a particular affirmative minor and a universal negative major, produces a particular negative, as in "some C is B, no B is A, therefore some C is not A." 91.5

The conclusions of this figure are self-evident. 91.6

The conditions of productivity in the second figure are that the two premises differ in quality, and that the major premise be universal; otherwise, we get discrepant conclusions revealing lack of productivity (which is a syllogism with true premises leading in some cases to an affirmative conclusion, and in others to a negative conclusion). 92

Its productive moods are also four. 93.1

The first, with two universals, the minor affirmative, produces a universal negative, as in "every C is B, no A is B; therefore, no C is A." This is proved by reductio, which involves joining the contradictory of the conclusion to the major to produce the contradictory of the minor. It can also be proved by conversion of the major premise to reduce it to the first figure. 93.2

The second, with two universals, the major affirmative, produces a universal negative, as in "no C is B, and every A is B; therefore, no C is A." This is proved by reductio, or by converting the minor, placing it as major, and converting the conclusion. 93.3

The third, with a particular affirmative minor and a universal negative major, produces a particular negative, as in "some C is B, no A is B, therefore some C is not A." This is proved by reductio, or by conversion of the major to 93.4

الأوّل وتفرض موضوع الجزئيّة د فكلّ د ب ولا شيء من ا ب فلا شيء من د ا ثمّ تقول بعض ج د ولا شيء من د ا فبعض ج ليس ا.

٥،٩٣ الرابع من سالبة جزئيّة صغرى وموجبة كلّيّة كبرى ينتج سالبة جزئيّة كقولنا بعض ج ليس ب وكلّ ا ب فبعض ج ليس ا بالخلف.

١،٩٤ وأمّا الشكل الثالث فشرطه موجبيّة الصغرى وإلّا لحصل الاختلاف وكلّيّة إحدى المقدّمتين وإلّا لكان البعض المحكوم عليه بالأصغر غير البعض المحكوم عليه بالأكبر فلم تجب التعدية.

٢،٩٤ وضروبه الناتجة ستّة.

٣،٩٤ الأوّل من موجبتين كلّيّتين ينتج موجبة جزئيّة كقولنا كلّ ب ج وكلّ ب ا فبعض ج ا بالخلف وهو ضمّ نقيض النتيجة إلى الصغرى لينتج نقيض الكبرى وبالردّ إلى الأوّل بعكس الصغرى.

٤،٩٤ الثاني من كلّيّتين والكبرى سالبة ينتج سالبة جزئيّة كقولنا كلّ ب ج ولا شيء من ب ا فبعض ج ليس ا بالخلف وبعكس الصغرى.

٥،٩٤ الثالث من موجبتين والكبرى كلّيّة ينتج موجبة جزئيّة كقولنا بعض ب ج وكلّ ب ا فبعض ج ا بالخلف وبعكس الصغرى وتفرض موضوع الجزئيّة د فكلّ د ب وكلّ ب ا فكلّ د ا ثمّ تقول كلّ د ج وكلّ د ا فبعض ج ا وهو المطلوب.

٦،٩٤ الرابع من موجبة جزئيّة صغرى وسالبة كلّيّة كبرى ينتج سالبة جزئيّة كقولنا بعض ب ج ولا شيء من ب ا فبعض ج ليس ا بالخلف وبعكس الصغرى والافتراض.

٧،٩٤ الخامس من موجبتين والصغرى كلّيّة ينتج موجبة جزئيّة كقولنا كلّ ب ج وبعض ب ا فبعض ج ا بالخلف وبعكس الكبرى وجعلها صغرى ثمّ عكس النتيجة والافتراض.

reduce it to the first figure. It can also be proved by ecthesis: expose the subject of the particular as D, then "every D is B, no A is B, therefore no D is A." But "some C is D, no D is A, therefore some C is not A."

The fourth, with a particular negative minor and a universal affirmative major, produces a particular negative, as in "some C is not B, and every A is B, therefore some C is not A." It is proved by reductio. 93.5

The conditions of productivity in the third figure are that the minor be affirmative (otherwise there will be discrepant conclusions), and that one of the premises be universal (otherwise the part of the middle of which the minor term is predicated may be different from the part of the middle of which the major is predicated, such that the judgment does not necessarily pass to the minor). 94.1

Its productive moods are six. 94.2

The first, with two universal affirmatives, produces a particular affirmative, as in "every B is C, and every B is A, therefore some C is A." It is proved by reductio (which involves conjoining the contradictory of the conclusion to the minor to produce the contradictory of the major), or by reduction to the first figure by converting the minor. 94.3

The second, with two universals, the major negative, produces a particular negative, as in "every B is C, and no B is A, therefore some C is not A." It is proved by reductio, or by converting the minor. 94.4

The third, with two affirmatives, the major universal, produces a particular affirmative, as in "some B is C, every B is A, therefore some C is A." It is proved by reductio, or by converting the minor, or by ecthesis: expose the subject of the particular premise as D. Then "every D is B, every B is A, therefore every D is A." Then we have "every D is C, every D is A, therefore some C is A"; and this is what is sought. 94.5

The fourth, with a particular affirmative minor and a universal negative major, produces a particular negative, as in "some B is C, no B is A, therefore some C is not A." It is proved by reductio, or by converting the minor, or by ecthesis. 94.6

The fifth, with two affirmatives, the minor universal, produces a particular affirmative, as in "every B is C, and some B is A, therefore some C is A." It is proved by reductio, or by using the converted major as minor and then converting the conclusion, or by ecthesis. 94.7

٨،٩٤ السادس من موجبة كلّيّة صغرى وسالبة جزئيّة كبرى ينتج سالبة جزئيّة كقولنا كلّ ب ج وبعض ب ليس ا فبعض ج ليس ا بالخلف والافتراض إن كانت السالبة مركّبة.

١،٩٥ وأمّا الشكل الرابع فشرطه بحسب الكمّيّة والكيفيّة إيجاب المقدّمتين مع كلّيّة الصغرى أو اختلافهما بالكيف مع كلّيّة إحداهما وإلّا لحصل الاختلاف الموجب لعدم الإنتاج.

٢،٩٥ وضروبه الناتجة ثمانية.

٣،٩٥ الأوّل من موجبتين كلّيّتين ينتج موجبة جزئيّة كقولنا كلّ ب ج وكلّ ا ب فبعض ج ا بعكس الترتيب ثمّ عكس النتيجة.

٤،٩٥ الثاني من موجبتين والكبرى جزئيّة ينتج موجبة جزئيّة كقولنا كلّ ب ج وبعض ا ب فبعض ج ا لما مرّ.

٥،٩٥ الثالث من كلّيّتين والصغرى سالبة ينتج سالبة كلّيّة كقولنا لا شيء من ب ج وكلّ ا ب فلا شيء من ج ا لما مرّ.

٦،٩٥ الرابع من كلّيّتين والصغرى موجبة ينتج سالبة جزئيّة كقولنا كلّ ب ج ولا شيء من ا ب فبعض ج ليس ا بعكس المقدّمتين.

٧،٩٥ الخامس من موجبة جزئيّة صغرى وسالبة كلّيّة كبرى ينتج سالبة جزئيّة كقولنا بعض ب ج ولا شيء من ا ب فبعض ج ليس ا لما مرّ آنفاً.

٨،٩٥ السادس من سالبة جزئيّة صغرى وموجبة كلّيّة كبرى ينتج سالبة جزئيّة كقولنا بعض ب ليس ج وكلّ ا ب فبعض ج ليس ا بعكس الصغرى لترتدّ إلى الثاني.

٩،٩٥ السابع من موجبة كلّيّة صغرى وسالبة جزئيّة كبرى ينتج سالبة جزئيّة كقولنا كلّ ب ج وبعض ا ليس ب فبعض ج ليس ا بعكس الكبرى لترتدّ إلى الثالث.

١٠،٩٥ الثامن من سالبة كلّيّة صغرى وموجبة جزئيّة كبرى ينتج سالبة جزئيّة كقولنا لا شيء من ب ج وبعض ا ب فبعض ج ليس ا بعكس الترتيب ثمّ عكس النتيجة.

The sixth, with a universal affirmative minor and a particular negative major, produces a particular negative conclusion, as in "every B is C, and some B is not A, therefore some C is not A." It is proved by reductio, or by ecthesis if the negative is compound. 94.8

The conditions for the fourth figure with respect to quantity and quality are that the two premises be affirmative and the minor a universal, or that the two premises differ from each other in quality and one of them be universal; otherwise, there will be discrepant conclusions, which reveal lack of productivity. 95.1

The productive moods in this figure come to eight. 95.2

The first, with two universal affirmatives, produces a particular affirmative, as in "every B is C, and every A is B, therefore some C is A." It is proved by reversing the order of the premises and converting the conclusion. 95.3

The second, with two affirmatives, the major being a particular, produces a particular affirmative, as in "every B is C, and some A is B, therefore some C is A." The proof is what preceded. 95.4

The third, with two universals, the minor being negative, produces a universal negative, as in "no B is C, and every A is B, therefore no C is A." The proof is what preceded. 95.5

The fourth, with two universals, the minor being affirmative, produces a particular negative, as in "every B is C, and no A is B; therefore, some C is not A." It is proved by converting both premises. 95.6

The fifth, with a particular affirmative minor and a universal negative major, produces a particular negative, as in "some B is C, and no A is B, therefore some C is not A." The proof is what preceded. 95.7

The sixth, with a particular negative minor and a universal affirmative major, produces a particular negative, as in "some B is not C, and every A is B, therefore some C is not A." This is proved by converting the minor to reduce it to the second figure. 95.8

The seventh, with a universal affirmative minor and a particular negative major, produces a particular negative, as in "every B is C, and some A is not B, therefore some C is not A." This is proved by converting the major to reduce it to the third figure. 95.9

The eighth, with a universal negative minor and a particular affirmative major, produces a particular negative, as in "no B is C, and some A is B, therefore some C is not A." It is proved by reversing the order of the premises and converting the conclusion. 95.10

٩٦ ويمكن بيان الخمسة الأوّل بالخلف وهو ضمّ نقيض النتيجة إلى إحدى المقدّمتين لينتج ماينعكس إلى نقيض الأخرى والثاني والخامس بالافتراض ولنبيّن ذلك في الثاني ليقاس عليه الخامس وليكن البعض الذي هوا د فكلّ د ا وكلّ د ب فنقول كلّ ب ج وكلّ د ب فبعض ج د وكلّ د ا فبعض ج ا وهو المطلوب.

٩٧ والمتقدّمون حصروا الضروب الناتجة في الخمسة الأولى وذكروا لعدم إنتاج الثلاثة الأخيرة الاختلاف في القياس من بسيطتين ونحن نشترط كون السالبة فيها من إحدى الخاصّتين فسقط ما ذكروه من الاختلاف.

الفصل الثاني في المختلطات

٩٨ أمّا الشكل الأوّل فشرطه بحسب الجهة فعليّة الصغرى.

٩٩ والنتيجة فيه كالكبرى إن كانت غير المشروطتين والعرفيّتين وإلّا فكالصغرى محذوفاً عنها قيد اللاضرورة واللادوام والضرورة المخصوصة بالصغرى إن كانت إحدى العامّتين وبعد ضمّ اللادوام اليها إن كانت إحدى الخاصّتين.

١٠٠ وأمّا الشكل الثاني فشرطه بحسب الجهة أمران أحدهما صدق الدوام على الصغرى أو كون الكبرى من القضايا المنعكسة السوالب والثاني أن لا تُستعمل الممكنة إلّا مع الضروريّة المطلقة أو مع الكبريين المشروطتين.

١٠١ والنتيجة دائمة إن صدق الدوام على إحدى مقدّمتيه وإلّا فكالصغرى محذوفاً عنها قيد اللادوام واللاضرورة والضرورة أيّة ضرورة كانت.

It is possible to prove the first five moods by reductio—that is to say, by joining the contradictory of the conclusion to one of the two premises to produce what converts to the contradictory of the other premise. The second and fifth moods can be proved by ecthesis. Let us prove this in the second; the fifth can be proved in the same way. Let the some that is A be D such that "every D is A" and "every D is B." Thus, "every B is C, every D is B, therefore some C is D" and "every D is A," so "some C is A"; this is what is sought. 96

The scholars who went before us limited the productive moods to the first five of this figure, and spoke of discrepant conclusions from a syllogism with two simple premises to show the lack of productivity of the last three. We, on the other hand, stipulate that the negative be one of the two specials, and then the problem they mention to do with discrepant conclusions falls away. 97

The Second Section: On Mixes of Modalized Premises

The condition for the first figure with regard to modality is that the minor premise be an actuality proposition. 98

If the major premise is not one of the two conditional propositions or the two conventionals, the conclusion has the modality of the major. If, on the other hand, the major is one of these four propositions, then (1) if the major is one of the two generals, the modality of the conclusion is like the minor, though dropping any restriction of non-perpetuity and nonnecessity, and whatever necessity belongs only to the minor; and (2) if the major is one of the two specials, the modality of the conclusion is like the minor, though joining the restriction of non-perpetuity to it.[34] 99

The condition for the second figure with regard to modality comes down to two matters. One of them is that the minor be true as a perpetual proposition, or that the major be one of the propositions with convertible negatives. The second is that the possible proposition is only used with an absolute necessary, or with either of the two conditional propositions as majors. 100

If one of the premises is true as a perpetual proposition, the conclusion is a perpetual proposition; otherwise, it is like the minor, but dropping its restriction of non-perpetuity or nonnecessity, and dropping whichever necessity the minor may have.[35] 101

١٠٢ وأمّا الشكل الثالث فشرطه فعليّة الصغرى والنتيجة كالكبرى إن كانت غير الأربع وإلّا فعكس الصغرى محذوفاً عنها اللادوام إن كانت الكبرى إحدى العامّتين ومضموماً إليها إن كانت إحدى الخاصّتين.

١٠٣ وأمّا الشكل الرابع فشرط إنتاجه بحسب الجهة أمور خمسة الأوّل كون القياس فيه من الفعليّات والثاني انعكاس السالبة المستعملة فيه والثالث صدق الدوام على صغرى الضرب الثالث أو العرفيّ العامّ على الكبرى الرابع كون الكبرى في السادس من المنعكسة السوالب الخامس كون الصغرى في الثامن إحدى الخاصّتين والكبرى ممّا يصدق عليها العرفيّ العامّ.

١٠٤ والنتيجة في الضربين الأوّلين عكس الصغرى إن صدق الدوام عليها أو كان القياس من الستّ المنعكسة السوالب وإلّا فمطلقة عامّة وفي الضرب الثالث دائمة إن صدق الدوام على إحدى مقدّمتيه وإلّا فعكس الصغرى وفي الرابع والخامس دائمة إن صدق الدوام على الكبرى وإلّا فعكس الصغرى محذوفاً عنه اللادوام وفي السادس كما في الثاني بعد عكس الصغرى وفي السابع كما في الثالث بعد عكس الكبرى وفي الثامن كعكس النتيجة بعد عكس الترتيب.

الفصل الثالث في الاقترانيّات الكائنة من الشرطيّات وهي خمسة أقسام

١٠٥ القسم الأوّل — ما يتركّب من المتّصلات والمطبوع منه ما كانت الشركة في جزء تامّ من المقدّمتين وتنعقد الأشكال الأربعة فيه لأنّه إن كان تالياً في الصغرى مقدّماً في الكبرى فهو الشكل الأوّل وإن كان تالياً فيهما فهو الشكل الثاني وإن كان مقدّماً

The condition for the third figure is that it have an actuality minor. The modality of the conclusion is like the major if the major is not one of the four descriptional propositions. Otherwise it is like the converse of the minor from which the restriction of non-perpetuity is dropped if the major is one of the two generals, and to which that restriction is added if the major is one of the two specials.[36] 102

The condition for productivity with respect to modality in the fourth figure comes down to five matters. The first is that the syllogism in this figure have actuality premises. The second is that the negative proposition used in it be convertible. The third is that, for the third mood, the minor be true as a perpetual proposition, or the major be true as a general conventional. The fourth is that the major in the sixth mood be a convertible negative. The fifth is that the minor of the eighth mood be one of the two specials, and the major be one of the propositions true as a general conventional. 103

The modality of the conclusion in the first two moods is that of the converse of the minor if (1) it is true as a perpetual proposition or (2) the syllogism is from the six propositions with convertible negatives; otherwise, it is a general absolute. In the third mood, the conclusion is a perpetual proposition if one of the premises is true as a perpetual proposition; otherwise, the modality is that of the converse of the minor. In the fourth and fifth moods, the conclusion is a perpetual proposition if the major is true as a perpetual proposition; otherwise, it is that of the converse of the minor, though dropping its restriction of non-perpetuity. In the sixth mood, it is like the second figure after converting the minor. In the seventh mood, it is like the third figure after converting the major. In the eighth mood, it is like the converse of the conclusion after reversing the order of the premises.[37] 104

The Third Section: On Connective Syllogisms with Hypothetical Premises

Containing five divisions

The First Kind This kind is compounded of conditional premises. The norm in this class is that in which what is shared is a complete part of both premises. The four figures are formed in it because, if the consequent in the minor is antecedent in the major, the syllogism is first figure; if the middle is consequent in both, the syllogism is second figure; if it is antecedent in both, the 105

فيهما فهو الشكل الثالث وإن كان مقدّماً في الصغرى تالياً في الكبرى فهو الشكل الرابع وشرائط الإنتاج وعدد الضروب والنتيجة في الكمّيّة والكيفيّة في كلّ شكل كما في الحمليّات من غير فرق مثال الضرب الأوّل من الشكل الأوّل كلّما كان ا ب فج د وكلّما كان ج د فه ز ينتج كلّما كان ا ب فه ز.

القسم الثاني ما يتركّب من المنفصلات والمطبوع منه ما كانت الشركة في جزء غير تامّ من المقدّمتين كقولنا إمّا كلّ ا ب أو كلّ ج د وإمّا كلّ د ه أو كلّ و ز ينتج إمّا كلّ ا ب أو كلّ ج ه أو كلّ و ز لامتناع خلوّ الواقع عن مقدّمتي التأليف وعن أحد الآخرين وتنعقد فيه الأشكال الأربعة والشرائط المعتبرة بين الحمليّتين معتبرة ههنا بين المتشاركين. ١٠٦

القسم الثالث ما يتركّب من الحمليّة والمتّصلة والمطبوع منه ما كانت الحمليّة كبرى والشركة مع تالي المتّصلة ونتيجته متّصلة مقدّمها مقدّم المتّصلة وتاليها نتيجة التأليف بين التالي والحمليّة كقولنا كلّما كان ا ب فكلّ ج د وكلّ د ه ينتج كلّما كان ا ب فكلّ ج ه وتنعقد فيه الأشكال الأربعة والشرائط المعتبرة بين الحمليّتين معتبرة ههنا بين التالي والحمليّة. ١٠٧

القسم الرابع ما يتركّب من الحمليّة والمنفصلة وهو على قسمين الأوّل أن تكون الحمليّات بعدد أجزاء الانفصال يشارك كلّ واحد منها واحداً من أجزاء الانفصال إمّا مع اتّحاد التأليفات في النتيجة كقولنا كلّ ج إمّا ب وإمّا د وإمّا ه وكلّ ب ط وكلّ د ط وكلّ ه ط ينتج كلّ ج ط لصدق أحد أجزاء الانفصال مع ما يشاركه من الحمليّة وإمّا مع اختلاف التأليفات في النتيجة كقولنا كلّ ج إمّا ب وإمّا د وإمّا ه وكلّ ب ج وكلّ د ط وكلّ ه ز ينتج كلّ ج إمّا ج وإمّا ط وإمّا ز لما مرّ. ١٠٨، ١

syllogism is third figure; and if it is antecedent in the minor and consequent in the major, the syllogism is fourth figure. The conditions of productivity, the number of moods, and the quantity and quality of the conclusion in every figure are exactly the same as in the categoricals, with no distinction. The form of the first mood is "whenever A is B, C is D, and whenever C is D, H is Z," which produces "whenever A is B, H is Z."

The Second Kind This kind is compounded of disjunctives. The norm in this class is that in which the two premises share an incomplete part, as in: "either every A is B or every C is D," and "either every D is H, or every W is Z," which produces "either every A is B or every C is H or every W is Z" (because of the inclusive disjunction arising from the two premises of the composition and one of the other two). The four figures are formed in this class, and the conditions taken into account between two categoricals are taken into account here between the two sharing a part. 106

The Third Kind This kind is compounded of a categorical and a conditional. The norm in this class is that in which the categorical is the major and the consequent of the conditional is shared. The conclusion is a conditional, the antecedent of which is the antecedent of the conditional premise, and the consequent is the conclusion of the composition between the consequent in the minor and the categorical, as in "whenever A is B, C is D," and "every D is H," which produces "whenever A is B, every C is H." So the four figures are formed in this class, and the conditions taken into account between two categoricals are taken into account here between the consequent and the categorical. 107

The Fourth Kind This kind is compounded of a categorical and a disjunctive, and forms two subcategories. In the first, the categorical propositions are the same in number as the parts of the disjunction, and each categorical proposition shares a term with one of the parts of the disjunction. Further, the compositions are either united in the conclusion, as in "every C is either B or D or H," and "every B is T and every D is T and every H is T," which produces "every C is T," because one of the parts of the disjunction is true along with a categorical with which it shares a term; or the compositions differ in the conclusion, as in "every C is either B or D or H; but every B is C and every D is T and every H is Z," which produces "every C is either C or T or Z," for the reason just mentioned. 108.1

والثاني أن تكون الحمليّات أقلّ من أجزاء الانفصال ولتكن الحمليّة واحدة والمنفصلة ٢،١٠٨
ذات جزئين والمشاركة مع أحدهما كقولنا إمّا كلّ ا ط أو كلّ ج ب وكلّ ب د ينتج إمّا كلّ ا ط أو كلّ ج د لامتناع خلوّ الواقع عن مقدّمتي التأليف وعن الجزء غير المشارك.

القسم الخامس ما يتركّب من المتّصلة والمنفصلة والاشتراك إمّا في جزء تامّ ١،١٠٩
من المقدّمتين أو غير تامّ منهما وكيف كان فالمطبوع منه ما تكون المتّصلة صغرى والمنفصلة موجبة كبرى مثال الأوّل قولنا كلّما كان ا ب فج د ودائمًا إمّا ج د أو ه ز مانعة الجمع ينتج دائمًا إمّا أن يكون ا ب او ه ز مانعة الجمع لاستلزام امتناع الاجتماع مع اللازم دائمًا أو في الجملة امتناعه مع الملزوم دائمًا أو في الجملة ومانعة الخلوّ تنتج قد يكون إذا لم يكن ا ب فه ز لاستلزام نقيض الأوسط للطرفين استلزامًا كلّيًا واستلزام ذلك المطلوب من الثالث مثال الثاني كلّما كان ا ب فكلّ ج د ودائمًا إمّا كلّ د ه أو و ز مانعة الخلوّ ينتج كلّما كان ا ب فإمّا كلّ ج ه أو و ز.
والاستقصاء في هذه الأقسام إلى الرسائل التي عملناها في فنّ المنطق. ٢،١٠٩

الفصل الرابع في القياس الاستثنائيّ

وهو مركّب من مقدّمتين إحداهما شرطيّة والأخرى وضع لأحد جزئيها أو رفعه ليلزم ١١٠
وضع الآخر أو رفعه ويجب إيجاب الشرطيّة ولزوميّة المتّصلة وكلّيّتها أو كلّيّة الوضع والرفع إن لم يكن وقت الاتّصال والانفصال هو بعينه وقت الوضع والرفع.

In the second, the categoricals are fewer than the parts of the disjunction. 108.2
Let the categorical be one, and the disjunctive have two parts, and the sharing takes place with one of those two parts, as in "either every A is T or every C is B," but "every B is D," which produces "either every A is T or every C is D," because an inclusive disjunction arises from the two premises of the composition and the unshared part.

The Fifth Kind This kind is compounded of a conditional and a disjunctive, 109.1
and what is shared is either a complete or an incomplete part of the premises. In either case, the norm is what has a conditional as minor and a disjunctive as affirmative major. An example of the first is "whenever A is B, C is D," but "always, either C is D or H is Z" (the disjunctive is an alternative denial), which produces "always, either A is B or H is Z" as an alternative denial, because the impossibility of conjunction with the implicate always or in general entails the impossibility of conjunction with the implicant always or in general. The disjunctive with an inclusive disjunction produces "sometimes, if A is not B then H is Z," due to the contradictory of the middle entailing the two extremes universally (and the inference of what is sought is by a third-figure syllogism). An example of the second kind—when the two premises have an incomplete part in common—is "whenever A is B, every C is D," and "always, either every D is H or W is Z" as an inclusive disjunction, which produces "whenever A is B, either every C is H or W is Z."

A full treatment of these divisions is given in the epistles we have written 109.2
on the art of logic.

The Fourth Section: On the Repetitive Syllogism

This is a compound of two premises, one a hypothetical, the other a propo- 110
sition that either affirms or denies one of the two parts of the hypothetical premise, such that affirming or denying the other part follows from it. It is necessary that the hypothetical premise is affirmative, and that the conditional is implicative and universal; or that the affirmation of the antecedent or denial of the consequent are universal (unless the time of the condition or disjunction is exactly the time of the affirmation or denial).

١١١ والشرطيّة الموضوعة فيه إن كانت متّصلة فاستثناء عين المقدّم ينتج عين التالي واستثناء نقيض التالي ينتج نقيض المقدّم وإلّا لبطل اللزوم دون العكس في شيء منهما لاحتمال كون التالي أعمّ من المقدّم وإن كانت منفصلة فإن كانت حقيقيّة فاستثناء عين أيّ جزء كان ينتج نقيض الآخر لاستحالة الجمع واستثناء نقيض أيّ جزء كان ينتج عين الآخر لاستحالة الخلوّ وإن كانت مانعة الجمع تنتج القسم الأوّل فقط لامتناع الاجتماع دون الخلوّ وإن كانت مانعة الخلوّ تنتج القسم الثاني فقط لامتناع الخلوّ دون الجمع.

الفصل الخامس في لواحق القياس
وهي أربعة

١١٢ الأوّل القياس المركّب وهو تركيب مقدّمات ينتج بعضها نتيجة يلزم منها ومن مقدّمة أخرى نتيجة أخرى وهلمّ جرًّا إلى أن يحصل المطلوب وهو إمّا موصول النتائج كقولنا كلّ ج ب وكلّ ب د فكلّ ج د ثمّ كلّ ج د وكلّ د ا فكلّ ج ا ثمّ كلّ ج ا وكلّ ا ه فكلّ ج ه أو مفصول النتائج كقولنا كلّ ج ب وكلّ ب د وكلّ د ا وكلّ ا ه فكلّ ج ه.

١١٣ والثاني قياس الخلف وهو إثبات المطلوب بإبطال نقيضه كقولنا لو كذب ليس كلّ ج ب لكان كلّ ج ب وكلّ ب ا على أنّها مقدّمة صادقة تنتج لو كذب ليس كلّ ج ب لكان كلّ ج ا لكن ليس كلّ ج ا على أنّه أمر محال فينتج ليس كلّ ج ب وهو المطلوب.

١١٤ الثالث الاستقراء وهو الحكم على كلّيّ لوجوده في أكثر جزئيّاته كقولنا كلّ حيوان يحرّك فكّه الأسفل عند المضغ لأنّ الإنسان والبهائم والسباع كذلك وهو لا يفيد اليقين لاحتمال أن لا يكون الكلّ بهذه الحالة كالتمساح.

If the hypothetical proposition that forms part of the repetitive syllogism is conditional, then the repetition of the antecedent produces exactly the consequent, and the repetition of the contradictory of the consequent produces the contradictory of the antecedent; otherwise, the implication would be void (though not in the reverse of either of the two cases above, due to the possibility that the consequent is more general than the antecedent). If the hypothetical is a disjunctive, then, if it is an exclusive disjunction, the repetition of either part produces the contradictory of the other due to the impossibility of conjunction; the repetition of the contradictory of either part produces the other, due to the impossibility of excluding both. If the disjunctive is alternative denial, it produces only in the first case (due to the impossibility of conjunction though not exclusion); and if the disjunctive is inclusive, it produces only in the second case (due to the impossibility of exclusion though not conjunction). 111

The Fifth Section: On Matters Appended to the Syllogism

Containing four topics

The first is the compound syllogism, which is compounded of several premises, some of which produce a conclusion, from which, along with another premise, follows another conclusion, and so on until what is sought is determined. The compound syllogism has either explicit intermediate conclusions, as in "every C is B, and every B is D, therefore every C is D," then "every C is D and every D is A, therefore every C is A," then "every C is A and every A is H, therefore every C is H"; or elided intermediate conclusions, as in "every C is B and every B is D and every D is A and every A is H, therefore every C is H." 112

The second is the reductio syllogism. What is to be proved is affirmed by disproving its contradictory, as in: Were "not every C is B" false, then "every C is B" and "every B is A" (on the basis that it is a true premise). This produces: Were "not every C is B" false, then "every C is A"; but it is not the case that "every C is A" (on the basis that it is something impossible); so this produces "not every C is B," which is what is sought. 113

The third is induction, which is a judgment on a universal made on the basis that it belongs to most of the particulars, as in "all animals move the lower jaw in eating because men, oxen, lions . . . do so." Induction does not convey certainty, because of the possibility that not all are like the ones considered (as, in this case, with the crocodile). 114

الرابع التمثيل وهو إثبات حكم في جزئيّ وُجد في جزئيّ آخر لمعنى مشترك بينهما ١١٥
كقولنا العالم مؤلّف فهو حادث كالبيت وأثبتوا عليّة المعنى المشترك بالدوران وبالتقسيم غير المردّد بين النفي والإثبات كقولهم علّة الحدوث إمّا التأليف أو كذا أو كذا والأخيران باطلان بالتخلّف فتعيّن الأوّل وهو ضعيف أمّا الدوران فلأنّ الجزء الأخير وسائر الشرائط مدار مع أنّها ليست بعلّة وأمّا التقسيم فالحصر ممنوع[١] لجواز عليّة غير المذكور وبتقدير تسليم عليّة المشترك في المقيس عليه لا تلزم عليّة في المقيس لجواز أن تكون خصوصيّة المقيس عليه شرطاً للعليّة أو خصوصيّة المقيس مانعة منـها.

١ (فالحصر ممنوع) في س، ف، ك؛ ت، ر: والحصر فممنوع.

The fourth is example, which is taking a judgment belonging to one par- 115
ticular and affirming it of another particular because of a meaning common to both, as in "the world is composed of parts, so it is produced in time, like a house." Proponents of this argument technique affirm the real causality of the common meaning by concomitance along with division (though this division is not the one that proceeds by opposing negation to affirmation), as in "the real cause of temporal production is either composition or this or that; yet the last two are false due to counterexample, so the first is specified." But this kind of argument is weak. The concomitance step in the argument is weak because the last part and the other conditions may be a presumed concomitant cause even though it is not a real cause. The division step in the argument is weak because its exhaustiveness may be rejected due to the possibility that the real causality belongs to something that has not been mentioned. Even supposing we grant the real causality of the common meaning in the principal analogue, its having real causality in the derivative analogue does not follow, due to the possibility that the specificities of the principal analogue are a condition for the causality, or the specificities of the derivative analogue are an impediment to such causality.

وأمّا الخاتمـة

ففيها بحثان

الأوّل في موادّ الأقيسـة

١،١١٦ وهي يقينيّات وغير يقينيّات أمّا اليقينيّات فستّ.

٢،١١٦ أوّليّات وهي قضايا تصوّر طرفيها كاف في الجزم بينهما كقولنا الكلّ أعظم من الجزء.

٣،١١٦ ومشاهدات وهي قضايا يُحكم بها لقوى ظاهرة أو باطنة كالحكم بأنّ الشمس مضيئة وأنّ لنا خوفاً وغضباً.

٤،١١٦ ومجرّبات وهي قضايا يُحكم بها لمشاهدات متكرّرة مفيدة لليقين كالحكم بأنّ شرب السقمونيا موجب للإسهال.

٥،١١٦ وحدسيّات وهي قضايا يُحكم بها لحدس قوي من النفس مفيد للعلم كالحكم بأنّ نور القمر مستفاد من الشمس والحدس هو سرعة الانتقال من المبادئ إلى المطالب.

٦،١١٦ ومتواترات وهي قضايا يُحكم بها لكثرة الشهادات بعد العلم بعدم امتناعها والأمن من التواطؤ عليها كالحكم بوجود مكّة وبغداد ولا ينحصر مبلغ الشهادات في عدد بل اليقين هو القاضي بكمال العدد.

٧،١١٦ والعلم الحاصل من التجربة والحدس والتواتر ليس بحجّة على الغير.

The Conclusion

Containing two discussions

The First Discussion: On Syllogistic Matters

These matters comprise what is certain and what is not. There are six propositions of certainty. 116.1

Primary propositions, which are propositions such that conceiving their two extremes is sufficient to be certain of the relation between the two, as in "the whole is greater than the part." 116.2

Observational propositions, which are propositions in which judgments are made by the external and internal faculties, like the judgment "the sun shines" and that we are subject to anger and fear. 116.3

Propositions based on experience, which are propositions in which judgments are made due to repeated observations conveying certainty, like "drinking scammony leads to diarrhea." 116.4

Intuited propositions, which are propositions in which judgments are made due to a strong intuition of the soul that conveys knowledge, like the judgment that the light of the moon is acquired from the sun. (Intuition is rapidity of transfer from principles to what is sought.) 116.5

Propositions based on sequential testimony, which are propositions in which judgments are made due to copious testimony, after it is known that the occurrence of what is claimed is not impossible, and they are trusted due to widespread agreement about them; this is like the existence of Mecca and Baghdad. There is no number set for the right level of testimony; rather, reaching certainty is what decides that the number is complete. 116.6

Knowledge available from the last three propositions (that is, those based on experience, intuition, or sequential testimony) does not constitute a proof that is compelling for someone else. 116.7

وقضايا قياساتها معها وهي التي يُحكم فيها بواسطة لا تغيب عن الذهن عند تصوّر حدودها كالحكم بأنّ الأربعة زوج لانقسامها بمتساويين. ٨،١١٦

والقياس المؤلّف من هذه الستّة يسمّى برهاناً وهي إمّا لمّيّ وهو الذي الحدّ الأوسط[1] فيه علّة للنسبة في الذهن والعين كقولنا هذا متعفّن الأخلاط وكلّ متعفّن الأخلاط محموم فهذا محموم وإمّا أنّيّ وهو الذي الحدّ الأوسط[2] فيه علّة للنسبة في الذهن فقط كقولنا هذا محموم وكلّ محموم متعفّن الأخلاط فهذا متعفّن الأخلاط. ١١٧

وأمّا غير اليقينيّات فستّ. ١،١١٨

مشهورات وهي قضايا يُحكم بها لاعتراف جميع الناس بها لمصلحة عامّة أو رقّة أو حميّة أو انفعالات من عادات وشرائع وآداب والفرق بينها وبين الأوّليّات أنّ الإنسان لو خُلّي ونفسَه مع قطع النظر عمّا وراء عقله لم يحكم بها بخلاف الأوّليّات كقولنا الظلم قبيح والعدل حسن وكشف العورة مذموم ومراعاة الضعفاء محمودة ومن هذه ما يكون صادقاً وما يكون كاذباً ولكلّ قوم مشهورات ولأهل كلّ صناعة بحسبها. ٢،١١٨

ومسلّمات وهي قضايا تتسلّم من الخصم فيبنى عليها الكلام لدفعه كتسليم الفقهاء مسائل أصول الفقه. ٣،١١٨

والقياس المؤلّف من هذين يسمّى جدلاً والغرض إقناع القاصر عن درك البرهان وإلزام الخصم. ٤،١١٨

ومقبولات وهي قضايا تؤخذ ممّن يُعتقد فيه إمّا لأمر سماويّ أو مزيد عقل ودين كالمأخوذات من أهل العلم والزهد. ٥،١١٨

ومظنونات وهي قضايا يُحكم بها اتّباعاً للظنّ كقولك فلان يطوف بالليل فهو سارق. ٦،١١٨

١ (الحدّ الأوسط) في ر، س، ف، ك؛ ت: حدّ الأوسط. ٢ (الحدّ الأوسط) في ف، ك؛ ت: حدّ الأوسط.

Implicitly syllogistic propositions, which are those in which judgment is made by an intermediary always present to the mind upon conceiving the terms, like the judgment that four is even due to its divisibility into two equal parts. 116.8

A syllogism composed of these six propositions of certainty is called a demonstration. It is either a demonstration of the reasoned fact, in which the middle term is a real cause for the relation between the terms of the conclusion in the mind and in concrete reality, as in "This person has putrid humors, everything with putrid humors is feverish, therefore this person is feverish"; or it is a demonstration of the fact, in which the middle term is a real cause for the relation in the mind alone, as in "This person is feverish, everything feverish has putrid humors, therefore this person has putrid humors." 117

Those that are not propositions of certainty are six. 118.1

Endoxic propositions, which are propositions in which the judgment is made because it is acknowledged by all people, whether on grounds of general utility, compassion, or fervor, or under the influence of customs or laws and manners. The distinction between these and primary propositions is that were a man taken out of a social context, ignoring everything that is not in the mind itself, he would not judge the endoxic to be true (in contrast to the primary); as in "injustice is evil," "justice is good," "uncovering the pudenda is blameworthy," "looking after the weak is praiseworthy." Some endoxic propositions are true, others not. Every nation has its own endoxic propositions, as do the exponents of every craft with respect to that craft. 118.2

Conceded propositions, which are propositions conceded by the opponent and upon which discourse is built to refute him, as in the way jurists concede questions in jurisprudence. 118.3

A syllogism composed of these last two kinds of premises is called dialectic. Its goal is to persuade someone who fails to grasp a demonstration, and to refute an opponent. 118.4

Received propositions, which are propositions taken up on the authority of someone credible, whether due to a heavenly matter or superior intellect or religiosity, as in what is taken from scholars and the pious. 118.5

Suppositional propositions, which are propositions in which judgments are made in accordance with a supposition, as in "so-and-so roams about at night, so he is a thief." 118.6

٧،١١٨ والقياس المؤلّف من هذين يسمّى خطابة الغرض منه ترغيب السامع فيما ينفعه من تهذيب الأخلاق وأمر الدين.

٨،١١٨ ومخيّلات وهي قضايا إذا وردت على النفس أثّرت فيها تأثيرًا عجيبًا من قبض وبسط كقولهم الخمر ياقوتة سيّالة والعسل مرّة متهوّعة.

٩،١١٨ والقياس المؤلّف منها يسمّى شعرًا والغرض منه انفعال النفس بالترغيب والتنفير ويروحه الوزن والصوت الطيّب.

١٠،١١٨ ووهميّات وهي قضايا كاذبة يحكم بها الوهم في أمور غير محسوسة كقولنا كلّ موجود مشار اليه ووراء العالَم فضاء لا يتناهى ولولا دفع العقل والشرائع لكانت من الأوّليّات وعُرف كذب الوهم بموافقته العقل في مقدّمات القياس الناتج لنقيض حكمه وإنكاره نفسه عند الوصول إلى النتيجة.

١١،١١٨ والقياس المؤلّف منها يسمّى سفسطة والغرض منها إفحام الخصم وتغليطه.

١١٩ والمغالطة قياس تفسد صورته بأن لا يكون على هيئة منتجة لاختلال شرط معتبر بحسب الكمّيّة أو الكيفيّة أو الجهة أو مادّته بأن تكون المقدّمة والمطلوب شيئًا واحدًا لكون الألفاظ مترادفة كقولنا كلّ إنسان بشر وكلّ بشر ضحّاك فكلّ إنسان ضحّاك أو كاذبة شبيهة بالصادقة من جهة اللفظ كقولنا لصورة الفرس المنقوش على الحائط هذا فرس وكلّ فرس صهّال لينتج أنّ تلك الصورة صهّالة أو من جهة المعنى لعدم مراعاة وجود الموضوع في الموجبة كقولنا كلّ إنسان وفرس فهو إنسان وكلّ إنسان وفرس فهو فرس لينتج بعض الإنسان فرس ووضع الطبيعيّة مكان الكلّيّة كقولنا الإنسان حيوان والحيوان جنس لينتج أنّ الإنسان جنس وأخذ الأمور الذهنيّة مكان العينيّة وبالعكس فعليك مراعاة كلّ ذلك لئلّا تقع في الغلط والمستعمل للمغالطة سوفسطائيّ إن قابل بها الحكيم ومشاغبيّ إن قابل بها الجدليّ.

A syllogism composed of these last two kinds of premises is called rhetoric. Its goal is to exhort the hearer to things useful for him, such as the cultivation of morals and religion. 118.7

Image-eliciting propositions, which are propositions that come upon the soul and have on it a marvelous influence such as melancholy and joy, as in "wine is a fluid ruby," and "honey is bitter and nauseous." 118.8

A syllogism composed of such propositions is called poetry, and its goal is to impress upon the soul a desire or dislike; it is animated by meter and a sweet voice. 118.9

Estimative propositions, which are false propositions, judgments made by the estimative faculty with respect to imperceptible matters, as in "every existent may be pointed to," and "beyond the world is a limitless void." Were they not refuted by reason or revelation they would pass for primary propositions. Their falsity can, however, be recognized, in that the estimative premise may agree with the intellect in premises of a syllogism, which then leads to the contradictory of the estimative judgment; the estimative faculty repudiates itself on arriving at the conclusion. 118.10

A syllogism formed of these is called sophistry, and its goal is to silence or deceive the opponent. 118.11

A fallacy is a syllogism whose form is corrupt such that it is not productive on account of a violation of some important condition in quantity, quality, or mode; or whose matter is corrupt such that the premise and the question may be identical due to synonymous expressions (as in "every man is a person, and every person is risible, therefore every man is risible"). Or one of the premises may be false but seem true with respect to expression, as when it is said of a painted horse: "every horse neighs, this is a horse, therefore the painting neighs." Or again, the falsity of the premises may be with respect to meaning, by failing for example to take care that the subject exists in the affirmative, as in "everything that is man-and-horse is man, and everything that is man-and-horse is horse," which produces "some men are horses"; or by using a natural proposition instead of a universal, as in "man is an animal, animal is a genus," which produces "man is a genus"; or by taking what is merely mental to be real (or vice versa). You should watch out for all these things to avoid falling into error. One who makes use of fallacies is called sophistical if he confronts a philosopher with them, and eristic if he confronts a dialectician with them.[38] 119

والبحث الثاني في أجزاء العلوم

١،١٢٠ وهي موضوعات وقد عرفتها ومبادئ[١] وهي حدود الموضوعات وأجزاؤها وأعراضها الذاتيّة والمقدّمات غير البيّنة في نفسها المأخوذة على سبيل الوضع كقولنا لنا أن نصل بين كلّ نقطتين بخطّ مستقيم وأن نعمل بأيّ بعد وعلى كلّ نقطة شئنا دائرة والمقدّمات البيّنة بنفسها كقولنا المقادر المساوية لمقدار واحد متساوية ومسائل وهي القضايا التي تطلب نسبة محمولاتها إلى موضوعاتها في ذلك العلم.

٢،١٢٠ وموضوعاتها قد تكون موضوع العلم كقولنا كلّ مقدار إمّا مشارك لآخر أو مباين وقد تكون هو مع عرض ذاتيّ كقولنا كلّ مقدار وسط في النسبة فهو ضلع ما يحيط به الطرفان وقد يكون نوعه كقولنا كلّ خطّ يمكن تنصيفه وقد يكون نوعه مع عرض ذاتيّ كقولنا كلّ خطّ قام على خطّ فإنّ زاويتي جنبيه إمّا قائمتان أو مساويتان لهما وقد يكون عرضاً ذاتيّاً كقولنا كلّ مثلّث فإنّ زواياه مساوية لقائمتين.

٣،١٢٠ وأمّا محمولاتها فخارجة عن موضوعاتها لامتناع أن يكون جزء الشيء مطلوباً ثبوته له بالبرهان.

وليكن هذا آخر الكلام في هذه الرسالة.

والحمد لله ربّ العالمين.

---

١ (مبادئ) في ف؛ ت، ر، س، ك: مباد.

The Second Discussion: On the Parts of the Sciences

The parts include the subjects (of which you have learned already); the principles, which include the definitions of the subjects and their parts and essential accidents, the premises that are not self-evident but accepted by way of being posited (as in "to connect any two points by a straight line" and "to produce a circle at any distance round any point"),[39] and the self-evident premises (as in "quantities equal to another quantity are equal to each other");[40] and the questions, which are propositions in which the relation of the predicates to their subjects in the respective science is sought. 120.1

The subjects of the questions are either identical with the subject of the science, as in "every magnitude is either commensurable or incommensurable with another magnitude"; or the subject with an essential accident, as in "every mean proportional is a side contained by the other two extremes"; or a species under the generic subject, as in "every line may be bisected"; or a species under the generic subject with an essential accident, as in "if one line is set upon another, the angles on either side are either two right angles or sum to two right angles"; or an essential accident, as in "every triangle has angles that sum to two right angles." 120.2

The predicates of the questions must be extrinsic to their subjects because it is impossible in a demonstration to seek to prove that a part of a given thing belongs to that thing. 120.3

Let this be the end of what we have to say in this epistle.
Praise be to God, Lord of the Worlds.

Notes

1 Asaph: The son of Berechiah the Gershonite (2 Chronicles 20:14); psalmist charged by King David to worship God in song and praise (1 Chronicles 15:16–17).

2 Q Fuṣṣilat 41:42.

3 "The rope of God," an allusion to Q Āl ʿImrān 3:103.

4 See Figure 1. The meaning on which an expression has been imposed contains (double solid line) the contained meaning, and implies (single solid line) the implicate meaning; the expression signifies by correspondence (dashed line) the meaning on which it has been imposed, by containment (dark dotted line) the contained meaning, and by implication (light dotted line) the implicate meaning.

5 Figure 2 sets out the dichotomous division in the lemma.

6 Among other meanings, the Arabic *ʿayn* is equivocal between "eye" and "spring."

7 Figure 3 sets out al-Ḥillī's dichotomous division given in comment on the lemma.

8 Figure 4 sets out an abbreviation of al-Rāzī's division, showing where synonymous terms fit. (Note that I use "synonymous" to translate *murādif* in §13, and reserve "univocal" for §12.1.)

9 Figure 5 sets out how al-Kātibī divides the predicables in §16.

10 Figure 6 gives a sample Porphyrian tree alluded to in §18.

11 Al-Kātibī is referring back to the division set out in §16 above.

12 Figure 7 presents the division of extrinsic properties according to the criteria of §22.2.

13 Figure 8 presents the division of universals in §24.

14 Figures 9 to 12 give Euler diagrams (taken from Keynes, *Studies and Exercises in Formal Logic*, 172) to illustrate the relations between terms set out in §26.

15 Figures 13 to 17 give Euler diagrams (taken from Keynes, *Studies and Exercises*, 172) to illustrate the relation between terms and their contradictory terms (complements) argued for in §27. (Note that §27.3 uses the example set out in Figure 14: ¬B and A overlap, but ¬A and B are disjunct; Figure 15 works with the example of overlap in §26.)

16 A reference to §15 above.

17 A reference to §16 above.

18 Figure 18 sets out the different kinds of expository phrases (*aqwāl shāriḥah*) in §36.

19 Figure 19 presents the division of propositions for §38 with §§39, 51, 60, and 61.

20 An allusion to a phrase in Q ʿAṣr 103:2.

21 Figures 20 and 21 present the implicational relations among the essentialist and externalist propositions as worked out by al-Kātibī's commentators on §47.

22 The Arabic for "inanimate" is a positive term (see §49).

23 Figure 22 sets out implicational relations among the simple propositions al-Kātibī presents, §52. Appendix 1 sets out the names of the thirteen propositions "customarily investigated," and Appendix 2 sets out all the propositions explicitly set out or implicitly referred to through the *Rules*.

24 Because I adopt Rescher's translations of the names of propositions, "conditional" is used both for the categorical necessity proposition under a descriptional reading and for the hypothetical proposition first set out in §39 above.

25 Examples of quantified hypothetical propositions given in Appendix 3.

26 Squares of opposition for $\mathbf{L}/\mathbf{M}_1$ and $\mathbf{A}_{D1}/\mathbf{X}_{D1}$ are given in Figures 24 and 25; further oppositions and entailments, including all four modalities in the referential reading (the *dhātī* reading), are given in Figure 26, and for the same modalities in the descriptional reading (the *waṣfī* reading) in Figure 27.

27 Contradictories are set out for both simple and compound propositions in Appendix 4.

28 Square of opposition for hypothetical propositions, limited to al-Kātibī's explicit formulation, in Figure 28.

29 See Table 1 for a summary of the conversions proved in §§73–80. Note the list of propositions given again before Table 1.

30 Figure 23 presents the implicational relations among the seven modalities whose e-propositions cannot be converted; the set of propositions is mentioned again in §83.

31 See Table 1 for a summary of the contrapositives proved in §§82–86.

32 For the propositions and their implicational relations, see Figure 23.

33 Claims in §87 are set out in Figures 29, 30, and 31.

34 See first-figure conclusions in Table 2.

35 See second-figure conclusions in Table 3.

36 See third-figure conclusions in Table 4.

37 See fourth-figure conclusions in Tables 5, 6, and 7 (I omit moods 6, 7, and 8).

38 An attempt is made to capture al-Kātibī's division of the fallacies as set out in his unedited *Jāmiʿ al-daqāʾiq* in Figure 32. Note the provisional nature of the diagram; I cannot see how to distinguish, for example, an argument's not being in a productive mood from its having a premise of the wrong quality.

39 This is what Euclid would call a postulate (his first and third postulates are given as examples).

40 This is one of Euclid's common notions (his first is the example).

Glossary

Abbasid caliphate (132–656/750–1258) caliphate that overthrew the Umayyad caliphate, ruling the Islamic empire from Baghdad, a city the second Abbasid caliph founded in 145/762. It was central to the cultural movement leading to the translation of philosophical and scientific texts from Greek into Arabic.

Abū ʿAbdallāh ibn Idrīs al-Shāfiʿī (d. 204/820) legal theorist and eponymous founder (or at least claimed founder) of the Shāfiʿī law school, to which al-Kātibī and most of his colleagues belonged.

Abū Bishr Mattā ibn Yūnus (d. 328/940) Nestorian Christian who translated and commented on Aristotle's works and played an important role in the translation of Peripatetic philosophy from Syriac into Arabic.

Abū Ḥāmid al-Ghazālī (d. 505/1111) Shāfiʿī lawyer and Ashʿarī theologian, famous for infusing rational traditions with mystical insights. He was a proponent of logic for proper theological and forensic reasoning.

Abū l-Ḥasan al-Ashʿarī (d. 324/936) theologian who responded to later representatives of the rationalist theologies that had gained official support in the first century of the Abbasid caliphate. He initiated a trend of cautious skepticism in Islamic theology. Al-Kātibī and most post-Avicennian thinkers who influenced his logic were trained in Ashʿarī theology.

Abū Naṣr al-Fārābī (d. 339/950) greatest philosopher writing in Arabic before Avicenna, credited by Avicenna with having clarified for him the purposes of Aristotle's *Metaphysics*. He is famous for commentaries on the *Organon*, and for independent works on logic, among other philosophical sciences.

Afḍal al-Dīn al-Khūnajī (d. 646/1248) logician from Azerbaijan who came to enjoy Ayyubid support, holding high judicial office in Cairo. His work *Kashf al-asrār ʿan ghawāmiḍ al-afkār* exercised great influence over al-Kātibī's logic.

ancients (al-qudamāʾ) term used by early philosophers in the Islamic world to refer to Greek philosophers from the earliest times up to late antiquity.

After the mid-seventh/mid-thirteenth century, the term was more typically used to refer to al-Fārābī and Avicenna.

Aristotle (d. 322 BC) Greek philosopher who wrote an influential series of works on logic, among other things. His books on logic came to be known collectively as the *Organon* ("instrument") and were translated into Arabic during the Abbasid era.

Asaph in the Hebrew Bible, son of Berechiah the Gershonite (2 Chronicles 20:14); psalmist charged by King David to worship God in song and praise (1 Chronicles 15:16–17).

Athīr al-Dīn al-Abharī (d. ca. 660/1261) teacher of al-Kātibī, perhaps also a colleague at the Marāghah observatory. His logic was subject to critical scrutiny by Naṣīr al-Dīn al-Ṭūsī.

Avicenna (Abū ʿAlī ibn Sīnā) (d. 428/1037) the greatest philosopher to write in Arabic. He was born in Bukhara, of Persian origin, and traveled extensively before taking his last position (as vizier) in Isfahan. His writings on logic have a status in the realms of Islam similar to that of Aristotle 's *Organon* in the Latin West.

Baghdad capital city of the Abbasid caliphate, founded in 145/762 on the banks of the Tigris River in Iraq. The city was sacked by the Īl-Khānid army in 656/1258, and took years to recover.

college (madrasah) an educational institution that became increasingly formalized through the early centuries of Islam. It became the prime center of learning in Muslim societies, especially from the late fifth/eleventh century (which is to say, in post-Avicennian Muslim society).

Euclid fourth century BC geometer, probably working in Alexandria. He wrote the *Elements*, a famous text on geometry, theorems of which are often alluded to by al-Kātibī and the commentators on *The Rules of Logic*. Geometry as developed in the *Elements* became the model for demonstrative science.

Fakhr al-Dīn al-Rāzī (d. 606/1210) Ashʿarī theologian, Shāfiʿī jurist, and philosopher from Rayy in Iran who rose to prominence in the eastern realms of Islam. One of the leading figures influencing al-Kātibī in the reinterpretation of Avicenna's philosophy.

Ibn al-Akfānī (d. ca. 748/1348) Kurdish encyclopedist, bibliographer, and physician who worked in Cairo.

Ibn Khaldūn (d. 808/1406) historian and polymath who produced a general theory of history and civilization in his most famous work, *al-Muqaddimah*. The work also contains a short but perceptive history of Arabic logic.

Ibn al-Muṭahhar al-Ḥillī (d. 726/1325) Shiʿi scholar from Iraq who studied logic with both Naṣīr al-Dīn al-Ṭūsī and Najm al-Dīn al-Kātibī. Overall, he seems—at least as a young scholar—to have had more sympathy with al-Ṭūsī's approach, and condemns various innovations of the *muta'akhkhirūn*. He was the author of what is almost certainly the earliest commentary on *The Rules of Logic*.

Īl-Khānid Empire (654-735/1256–1335) khanate of the Mongol Empire, centered on the lands of Iran.

Marāghah ancient city in northwest Iran, approximately sixty miles (one hundred kilometers) south of Tabrīz. It was the residence of early Īl-Khānid rulers, and the site of a large astronomical observatory whose construction began in 657/1259.

muḥaqqiqūn term meaning "verifying [scholars]," later used to distinguish Avicennian purists like Naṣīr al-Dīn al-Ṭūsī from the *muta'akhkhirūn* in the sense of Rāzian revisionists.

muta'akhkhirūn term meaning "later scholars," first used to refer to scholars coming a considerable time after Aristotle in late antiquity, later used to refer to scholars coming after Avicenna. The term may be used with overtones of an Avicennian revisionism; al-Rāzī is often referred to as a leading scholar among the *muta'akhkhirūn*.

mutaqaddimūn term meaning "early scholars," first used to refer to Aristotle, his predecessors, and his successors into early late antiquity, later often used to refer to Avicenna and his predecessors.

Najm al-Dīn al-Kātibī (d. 675/1276) logician and astronomer from Qazvīn who studied under Athīr al-Dīn al-Abharī, worked in the Marāghah observatory, and wrote long commentaries on logic texts by Fakhr al-Dīn al-Rāzī and Afḍal al-Dīn al-Khūnajī. He was the author of the *Rules of Logic*.

Naṣīr al-Dīn al-Ṭūsī (d. 672/1274) polymath, astronomer and influential Avicennian philosopher from Ṭūs, sent by the Īl-Khānid rulers to found the Marāghah observatory. He was a senior colleague of al-Kātibī and teacher of al-Ḥillī; he also wrote critical responses to works by Fakhr al-Dīn al-Rāzī.

Organon collective title for Aristotle's works on logic, taken in the Arabic tradition to include *Categories, De Interpretatione, Prior Analytics, Posterior Analytics, Topics, Sophistical Refutations,* the *Rhetoric,* and the *Poetics.* Porphyry's *Introduction* prefaced the collection.

Peter of Spain logician active in Europe in the thirteenth century, contemporary with al-Kātibī, and author of a hugely popular treatise on logic, the *Summaries of Logic.*

Porphyry (d. AD 305) Neoplatonic philosopher from Tyre, student and editor of Plotinus. He wrote the *Introduction,* a widely read introduction to the five universals used in logic.

Qazvīn city near the southern shores of the Caspian Sea, nearly three hundred miles (five hundred kilometers) from Tabrīz, and birthplace of al-Kātibī.

Quṭb al-Dīn al-Rāzī al-Taḥtānī (d. 766/1365) logician from near Rayy in Iran who studied with Ibn al-Muṭahhar al-Ḥillī. He traveled west, settling in Damascus toward the end of his life, and is famous for writing what is perhaps the most widely used commentary on *The Rules of Logic.*

Saʿd al-Dīn al-Taftāzānī (d. 792/1390) theologian and logician from Khurasan who worked at various eastern courts, ultimately dying in Tamerlane's capital Samarqand. He conducted a scholarly feud with al-Sayyid al-Sharīf al-Jurjānī, and was author of a commentary aimed at correcting aspects of Quṭb al-Dīn al-Rāzī al-Taḥtānī's commentary on *The Rules of Logic.*

al-Sayyid al-Sharīf al-Jurjānī (d. 816/1413) scholar brought as a young man by Saʿd al-Dīn al-Taftāzānī to Samarqand, where al-Jurjānī quickly became al-Taftāzānī's rival. He was the author of marginal notes on *The Rules of Logic.*

Shams al-Dīn al-Juwaynī (d. 683/1284) Persian statesman and patron of the arts and sciences. *The Rules of Logic* is dedicated to him and his brother Bahāʾ al-Dīn.

Tabrīz capital of the Īl-Khānid khanate after Marāghah. It was sacked at the end of the eighth/fourteenth century by Tamerlane.

Umayyad caliphate (41–132/661–750) the first caliphal dynasty, following the initial four caliphs, known as the Rightly Guided Caliphs. The Umayyads shifted the administrative center of the Islamic world to Damascus, and early translations from Greek began under their rule.

Tables

Key to Symbols for Propositions

Both versions of al-Taḥtānī's *Redaction* I use have some problems in the tables they present for the conclusions to syllogisms with mixed modal premises, and I have instead adopted the tables in Ibn Mubārakshāh's commentary on the *Rules*. I am grateful to Khaled El-Rouayheb for alerting me to the value of this work and offering me a manuscript of it; and to Dustin Klinger for overcoming my reluctance to consult yet another commentator: Ibn Mubārakshāh, *Sharḥ al-Shamsiyyah* (El-Rouayheb, "Two Fourteenth-Century Islamic Philosophers: Ibn Mubārakshāh al-Bukhārī and Mullāzāde al-Kharziyānī," 4n10). The tables appear, in the order I give them below, on folios 96a, 98b, 99b, 102a, 102b, and 103a. I list again most of the propositional types given in Appendix 2; unlike the list in Appendix 2, however, I here follow the order Ibn Mubārakshāh adopts in setting out the major and minor premises in the tables.

L	necessary (*al-ḍarūriyyah*)
A	perpetual (*al-dā'imah*)
$\mathbf{L}_{\mathbf{D1}}$	general conditional (*al-mashrūṭah al-ʿāmmah*)
$\mathbf{A}_{\mathbf{D1}}$	general conventional (*al-ʿurfiyyah al-ʿāmmah*)
$\mathbf{L}_{\mathbf{D2}}$	special conditional (*al-mashrūṭah al-khāṣṣah*)
$\mathbf{A}_{\mathbf{D2}}$	special conventional (*al-ʿurfiyyah al-khāṣṣah*)
$\mathbf{X}_{1}$	general absolute (*al-muṭlaqah al-ʿāmmah*)
$\mathbf{L}_{\mathbf{T2}}$	temporal (*al-waqtiyyah*)
$\mathbf{L}_{\mathbf{X2}}$	spread (*al-muntashirah*)
$\mathbf{X}_{2}$	non-perpetual existential (*al-wujūdiyyah al-lā-dā'imah*)
$\mathbf{X}_{\sim\mathbf{L}}$	nonnecessary existential (*al-wujūdiyyah al-lā-ḍarūriyyah*)
$\mathbf{M}_{1}$	general possible (*al-mumkinah al-ʿāmmah*)

Simple propositions not customarily investigated that come up:

$\mathbf{L}_{\mathbf{T1}}$	absolute temporal (*al-waqtiyyah al-muṭlaqah*)
$\mathbf{L}_{\mathbf{X1}}$	absolute spread (*al-muntashirah al-muṭlaqah*)

$\mathbf{X}_{T1}$	temporal absolute (*al-muṭlaqah al-waqtiyyah*)
$\mathbf{X}_{X1}$	spread absolute (*al-muṭlaqah al-muntashirah*)
$\mathbf{X}_{D1}$	absolute continuing (*al-ḥīniyyah al-muṭlaqah*)

Compound propositions not customarily investigated that come up:

$\mathbf{L}_2$	non-perpetual necessary (impossible proposition) (*al-ḍarūriyyah al-lā-dā'imah*)
$\mathbf{A}_2$	non-perpetual perpetual (impossible proposition) (*al-dā'imah al-lā-dā'imah*)
$\mathbf{A}_{D(2)}$	non-perpetual-for-some conventional (*al-ʿurfiyyah al-lā-dā'imah fī l-baʿḍ*)
$\mathbf{X}_{T2}$	non-perpetual temporal absolute (*al-muṭlaqah al-waqtiyyah al-lā-dā'imah*)
$\mathbf{X}_{X2}$	non-perpetual spread absolute (*al-muṭlaqah al-muntashirah al-lā-dā'imah*)
$\mathbf{X}_{D2}$	non-perpetual absolute continuing (*al-ḥīniyyah al-muṭlaqah al-lā-dā'imah*)

Table 1: Conversion and Contraposition

E conversion	**A contraposition (a → e)**
$\mathbf{L} \to \mathbf{A}$ (§75)	$\mathbf{L} \to \mathbf{A}$ (§83.2)
$\mathbf{A} \to \mathbf{A}$ (§75)	$\mathbf{A} \to \mathbf{A}$ (§83.2)
$\mathbf{L}_{D1} \to \mathbf{A}_{D1}$ (§76.1)	$\mathbf{L}_{D1} \to \mathbf{A}_{D1}$ (§83.3)
$\mathbf{A}_{D1} \to \mathbf{A}_{D1}$ (§76.1)	$\mathbf{A}_{D1} \to \mathbf{A}_{D1}$ (§83.3)
$\mathbf{L}_{D2} \to \mathbf{A}_{D(2)}$ (§76.2)	$\mathbf{L}_{D2} \to \mathbf{A}_{D(2)}$ (§83.4)
$\mathbf{A}_{D2} \to \mathbf{A}_{D(2)}$ (§76.2)	$\mathbf{A}_{D2} \to \mathbf{A}_{D(2)}$ (§83.4)

O conversion	**I contraposition (i → o)**
$\mathbf{L}_{D2} \to \mathbf{A}_{D2}$ (§77)	$\mathbf{L}_{D2} \to \mathbf{A}_{D2}$ (§84.1)
$\mathbf{A}_{D2} \to \mathbf{A}_{D2}$ (§77)	$\mathbf{A}_{D2} \to \mathbf{A}_{D2}$ (§84.1)

A/I conversion	**E/O contraposition (e → i)**
$\mathbf{L} \to \mathbf{X}_{D1}$ (§78.1)	**L** fails (§86)
$\mathbf{A} \to \mathbf{X}_{D1}$ (§78.1)	**A** fails (§86)
$\mathbf{L}_{D1} \to \mathbf{X}_{D1}$ (§78.1)	$\mathbf{L}_{D1}$ fails (§86)
$\mathbf{A}_{D1} \to \mathbf{X}_{D1}$ (§78.1)	$\mathbf{A}_{D1}$ fails (§86)
$\mathbf{L}_{D2} \to \mathbf{X}_{D2}$ (§78.2 for a, §78.3 for i)	$\mathbf{L}_{D2} \to \mathbf{X}_{D1}$ (§85.1)
$\mathbf{A}_{D2} \to \mathbf{X}_{D2}$ (§78.2 for a, §78.3 for i)	$\mathbf{A}_{D2} \to \mathbf{X}_{D1}$ (§85.1)
$\mathbf{X}_1 \to \mathbf{X}_1$ (§78.4)	$\mathbf{X}_1$ fails (§86)
$\mathbf{L}_{T2} \to \mathbf{X}_1$ (§78.4)	$\mathbf{L}_{T2} \to \mathbf{X}_1$ (§85.2)
$\mathbf{L}_{X2} \to \mathbf{X}_1$ (§78.4)	$\mathbf{L}_{X2} \to \mathbf{X}_1$ (§85.2)
$\mathbf{X}_2 \to \mathbf{X}_1$ (§78.4)	$\mathbf{X}_2 \to \mathbf{X}_1$ (§85.2)
$\mathbf{X}_{\sim L} \to \mathbf{X}_1$ (§78.4)	$\mathbf{X}_{\sim L} \to \mathbf{X}_1$ (§85.2)
$\mathbf{M}_1$ fails (§80)	$\mathbf{M}_1$ fails (§86)
$\mathbf{M}_2$ fails (§80)	$\mathbf{M}_2$ fails (§86)

Table 2: Figure 1 Mixes

Major ⟶ (columns); ⟵ Minor (rows)

	L_{D1}	A_{D1}	L_{D2}	A_{D2}
L	L	A	L_2 *	A_2 *
A	A	A	A_2 *	A_2 *
L_{D1}	L_{D1}	A_{D1}	L_{D2}	A_{D2}
A_{D1}	A_{D1}	A_{D1}	A_{D2}	A_{D2}
L_{D2}	L_{D1}	A_{D1}	L_{D2}	A_{D2}
A_{D2}	A_{D1}	A_{D1}	A_{D2}	A_{D2}
X_1	X_1	X_1	X_2	X_2
L_{T2}	L_{T1}	X_{T1}	L_{T2}	X_{T2}
L_{X2}	L_{X1}	X_{X1}	L_{X2}	X_{X2}
X_2	X_1	X_1	X_2	X_2
$X_{\sim L}$	X_1	X_1	X_2	X_2

* = impossible.

Table 3: Figure 2 Mixes

Major ⟶ (columns); ⟵ Minor (rows)

	L	L_{D1}	L_{D2}	A	A_{D1}	A_{D2}	X_1	L_{T2}	L_{X2}	X_2	$X_{\sim L}$	M_1	M_2
L	A	A	A	A	A	A	A	A	A	A	A	A	A
A	A	A	A	A	A	A	A	A	A	A	A		
L_{D1}	A	A_{D1}	A_{D1}	A	A_{D1}	A_{D1}							
A_{D1}	A	A_{D1}	A_{D1}	A	A_{D1}	A_{D1}							
L_{D2}	A	A_{D1}	A_{D1}	A	A_{D1}	A_{D1}							
A_{D2}	A	A_{D1}	A_{D1}	A	A_{D1}	A_{D1}							
X_1	A	X_1	X_1	A	X_1	X_1							
L_{T2}	A	X_{T1}	X_{T1}	A	X_{T1}	X_{T1}							
L_{X2}	A	X_{X1}	X_{X1}	A	X_{X1}	X_{X1}							
X_2	A	X_1	X_1	A	X_1	X_1							
$X_{\sim L}$	A	X_1	X_1	A	X_1	X_1							
M_1	A	M_1	M_1										

Table 4: Figure 3 Mixes

↓ Minor \ Major ⟶	L_{D1}	A_{D1}	L_{D2}	A_{D2}
L	X_{D1}	X_{D1}	X_{D2}	X_{D2}
A	X_{D1}	X_{D1}	X_{D2}	X_{D2}
L_{D1}	X_{D1}	X_{D1}	X_{D2}	X_{D2}
A_{D1}	X_{D1}	X_{D1}	X_{D2}	X_{D2}
L_{D2}	X_{D1}	X_{D1}	X_{D2}	X_{D2}
A_{D2}	X_{D1}	X_{D1}	X_{D2}	X_{D2}
X_1	X_1	X_1	X_2	X_2
L_{T2}	X_1	X_1	X_2	X_2
L_{X2}	X_1	X_1	X_2	X_2
X_2	X_1	X_1	X_2	X_2
$X_{\sim L}$	X_1	X_1	X_2	X_2

Table 5: Figure 4, Bramantip and Dimaris

↓ Minor \ Major ⟶	L	A	L_{D1}	A_{D1}	L_{D2}	A_{D2}	X_1	L_{T2}	L_{X2}	X_2	$X_{\sim L}$
L	X_{D1}	X_{D1}	X_{D1}	X_{D1}	X_{D1}	X_{D1}	X_{D1}	X_{D1}	X_{D1}	X_{D1}	X_{D1}
A	X_{D1}	X_{D1}	X_{D1}	X_{D1}	X_{D1}	X_{D1}	X_{D1}	X_{D1}	X_{D1}	X_{D1}	X_{D1}
L_{D1}	X_{D1}	X_{D1}	X_{D1}	X_{D1}	X_{D1}	X_{D1}	X_1	X_1	X_1	X_1	X_1
A_{D1}	X_{D1}	X_{D1}	X_{D1}	X_{D1}	X_{D1}	X_{D1}	X_1	X_1	X_1	X_1	X_1
L_{D2}	X_{D2}	X_{D2}	X_{D2}	X_{D2}	X_{D2}	X_{D2}	X_1	X_1	X_1	X_1	X_1
A_{D2}	X_{D2}	X_{D2}	X_{D2}	X_{D2}	X_{D2}	X_{D2}	X_1	X_1	X_1	X_1	X_1
X_1	X_1	X_1	X_1	X_1	X_1	X_1	X_1	X_1	X_1	X_1	X_1
L_{T2}	X_1	X_1	X_1	X_1	X_1	X_1	X_1	X_1	X_1	X_1	X_1
L_{X2}	X_1	X_1	X_1	X_1	X_1	X_1	X_1	X_1	X_1	X_1	X_1
X_2	X_1	X_1	X_1	X_1	X_1	X_1	X_1	X_1	X_1	X_1	X_1
$X_{\sim L}$	X_1	X_1	X_1	X_1	X_1	X_1	X_1	X_1	X_1	X_1	X_1

Table 6: Figure 4, Camenes

Major ⟶ ; ⟵ Minor

	L	A	L_{D1}	A_{D1}	L_{D2}	A_{D2}	X_1	L_{T2}	L_{X2}	X_2	$X_{\sim L}$
L	**A**	**A**	**A**	**A**	**A**	**A**	**A**	**A**	**A**	**A**	**A**
A	**A**	**A**	**A**	**A**	**A**	**A**	**A**	**A**	**A**	**A**	**A**
L_{D1}	**A**	**A**	A_{D1}	A_{D1}	A_{D1}	A_{D1}					
A_{D1}	**A**	**A**	A_{D1}	A_{D1}	A_{D1}	A_{D1}					
L_{D2}	**A**	**A**	$A_{D(2)}$	$A_{D(2)}$	$A_{D(2)}$	$A_{D(2)}$					
A_{D2}	**A**	**A**	$A_{D(2)}$	$A_{D(2)}$	$A_{D(2)}$	$A_{D(2)}$					

Table 7: Figure 4, Fesapo and Fresison

Major ⟶ ; ⟵ Minor

	L	A	L_{D1}	A_{D1}	L_{D2}	A_{D2}
L	**A**	**A**	X_{D1}	X_{D1}	X_{D1}	X_{D1}
A	**A**	**A**	X_{D1}	X_{D1}	X_{D1}	X_{D1}
L_{D1}	**A**	**A**	X_{D1}	X_{D1}	X_{D1}	X_{D1}
A_{D1}	**A**	**A**	X_{D1}	X_{D1}	X_{D1}	X_{D1}
L_{D2}	**A**	**A**	X_{D1}	X_{D1}	X_{D1}	X_{D1}
A_{D2}	**A**	**A**	X_{D1}	X_{D1}	X_{D1}	X_{D1}
X_1	**A**	**A**	X_1	X_1	X_1	X_1
L_{T2}	**A**	**A**	X_1	X_1	X_1	X_1
L_{X2}	**A**	**A**	X_1	X_1	X_1	X_1
X_2	**A**	**A**	X_1	X_1	X_1	X_1
$X_{\sim L}$	**A**	**A**	X_1	X_1	X_1	X_1

Figures

Figure 1: The tripartite signification (for §7)

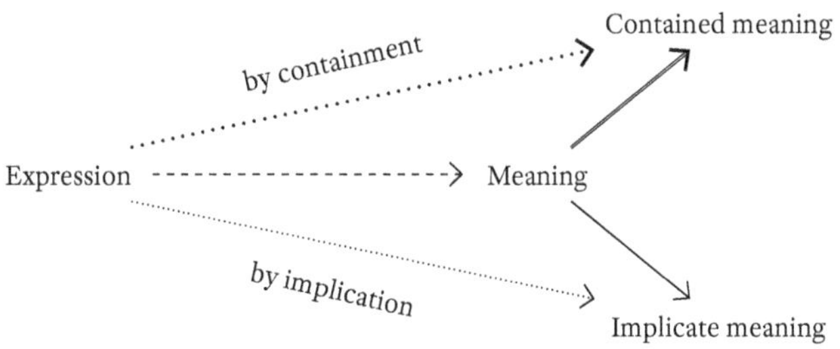

Figure 2: The parts of speech (for §11)

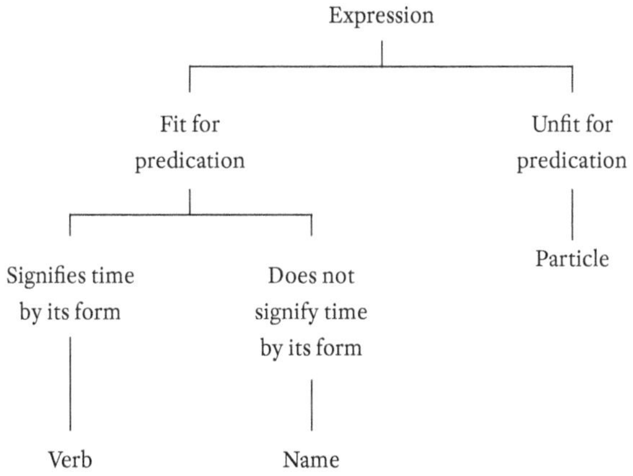

Figure 3: Al-Ḥillī on the relation of expression to meaning (for §12)

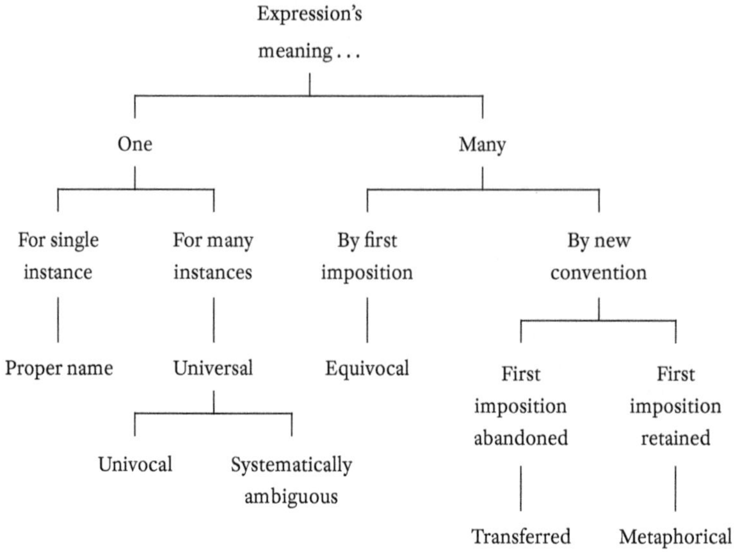

Figure 4: Al-Rāzī on the relation of expression to meaning (for §§12 and 13)

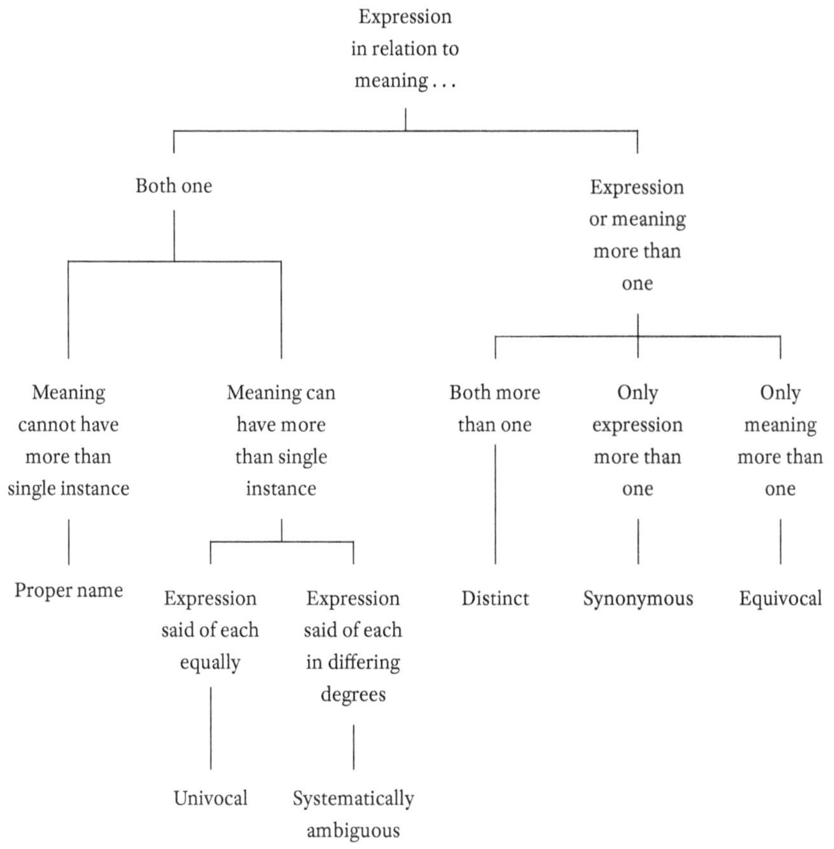

Figure 5: Division of the predicables (for §16)

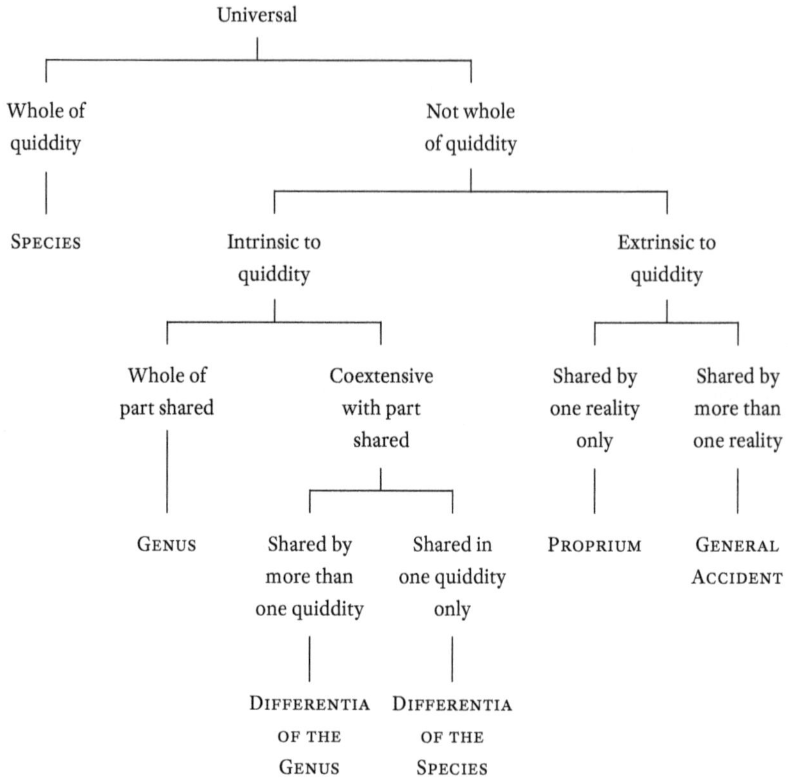

Figure 6: Porphyrian tree (for §18)

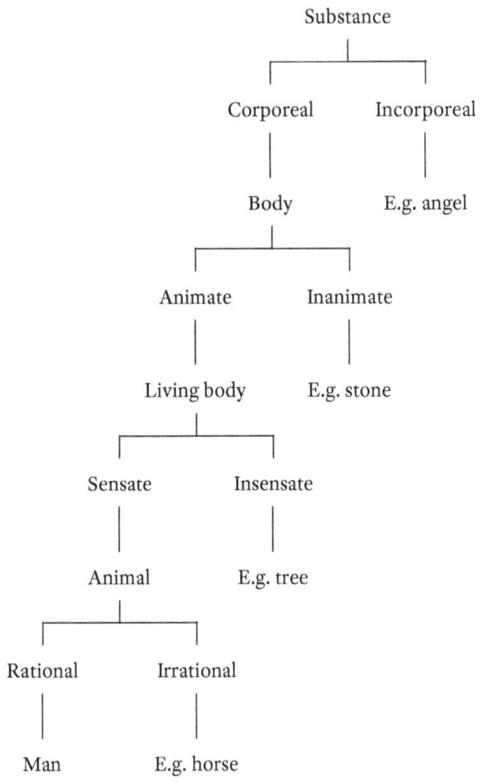

Figure 7: Separable and inseparable (for §22)

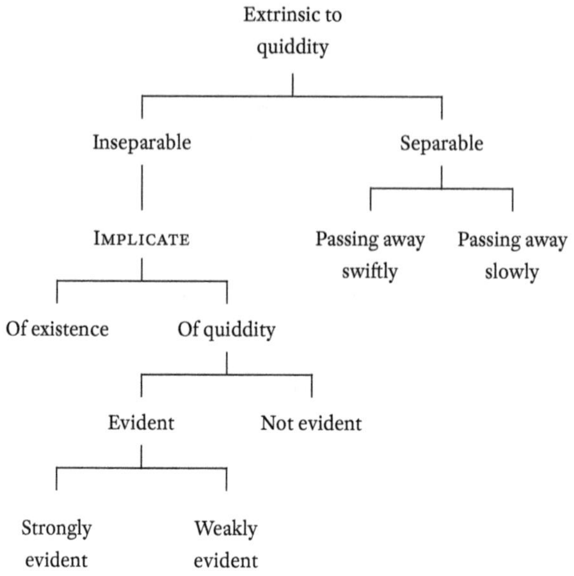

Figure 8: Universals and existence (for §24)

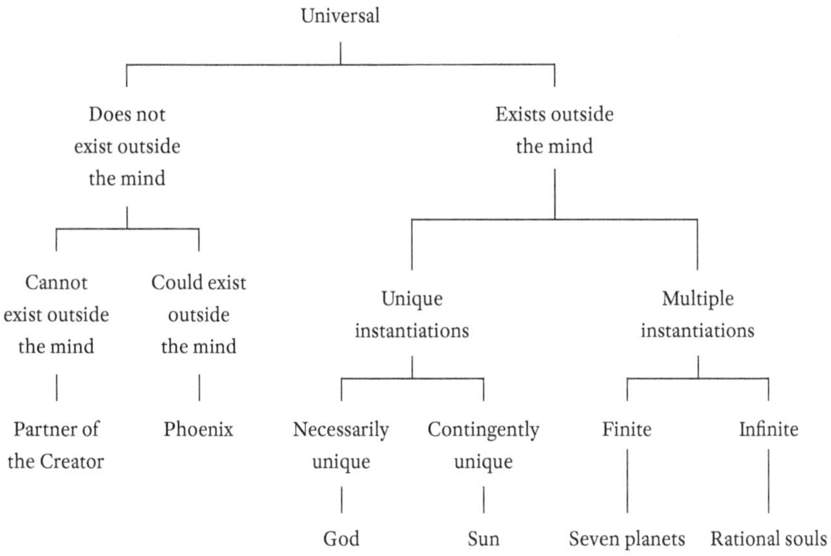

Figure 9: Coextensive terms (for §26)

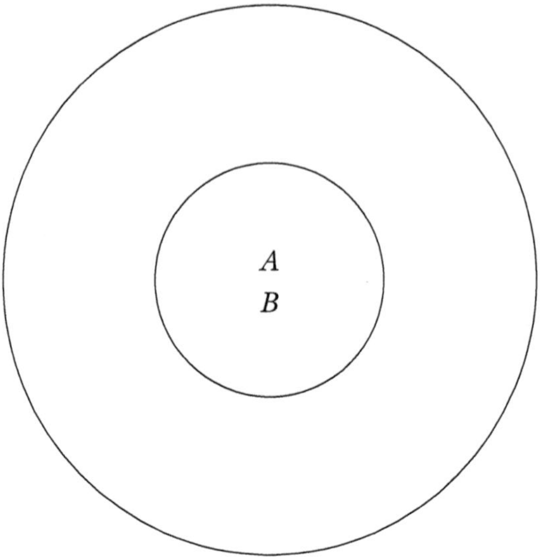

Figure 10: One term included in the other (for §26)

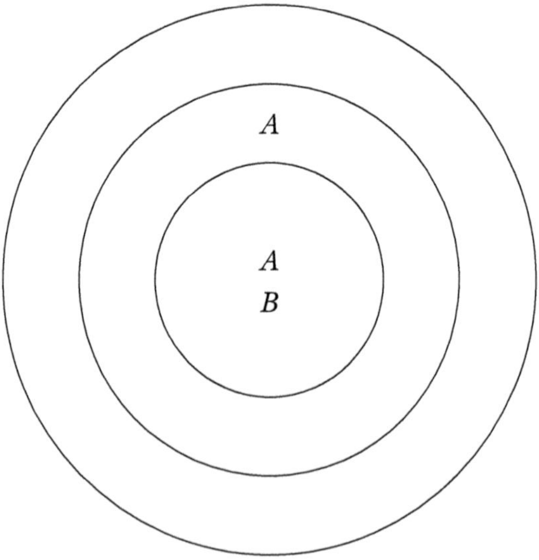

Figure 11: Overlapping terms (for §26)

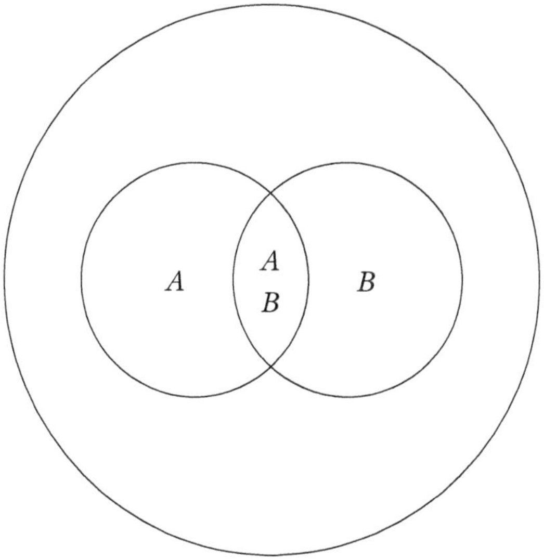

Figure 12: Disjoined terms (for §26)

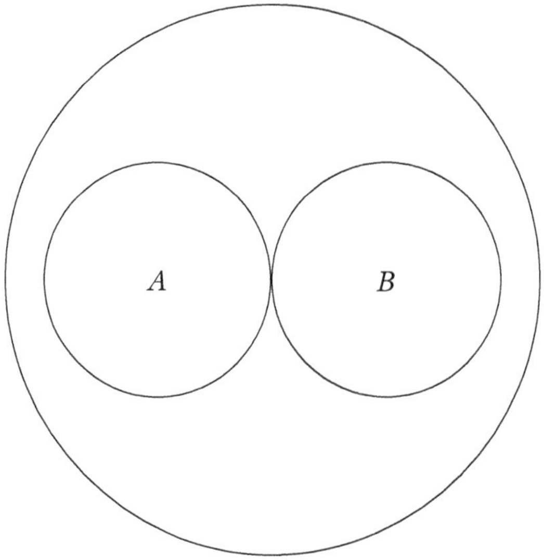

Figure 13: Contradictories of coextensive terms (for §27)

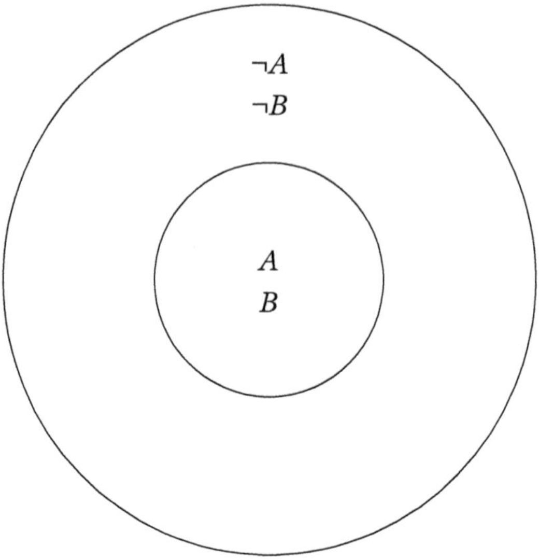

Figure 14: Contradictories of terms, one included in the other (for §27)

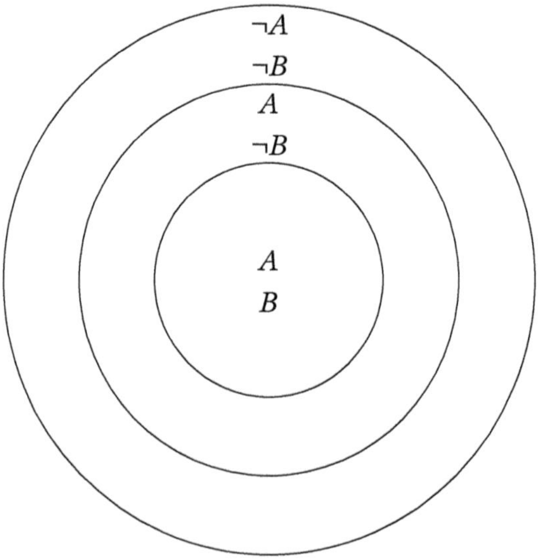

Figure 15: Contradictories of overlapping terms (for §27)

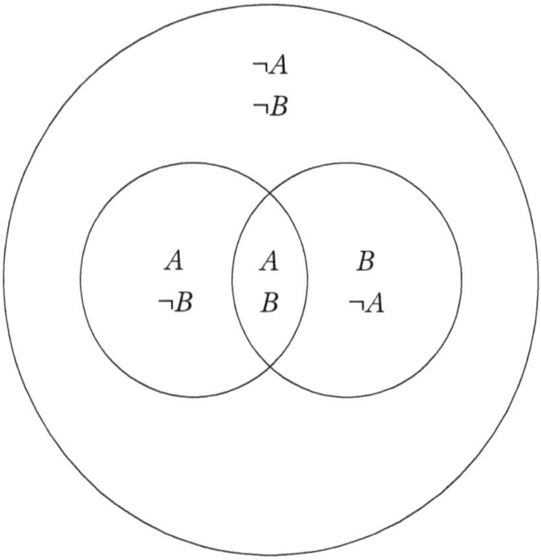

Figure 16: Contradictories of two disjoined terms, case 1 (for §27)

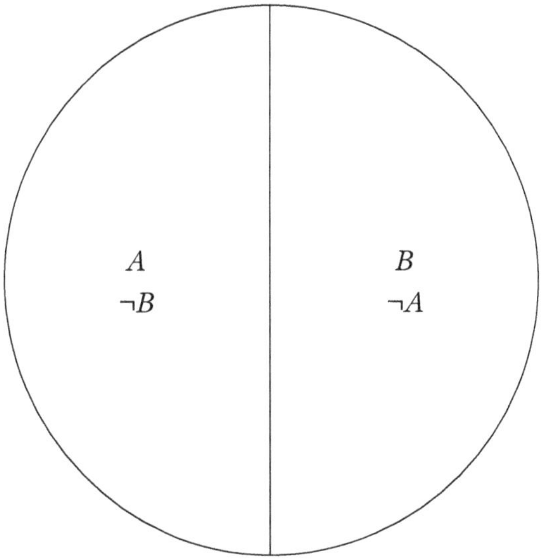

Figure 17: Contradictories of two disjoined terms, case 2 (for §27)

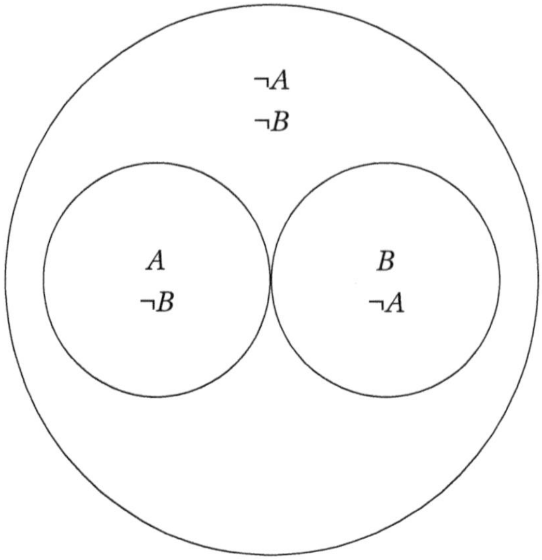

Figure 18: Al-Kātibī on definitions and delineations (for §36)

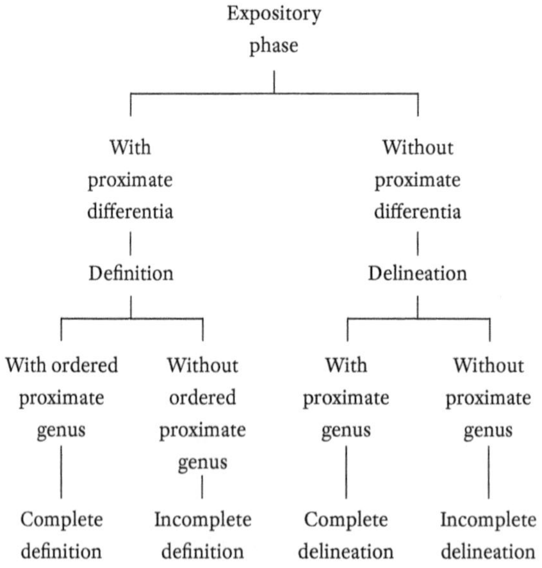

Figure 19: Species of propositions

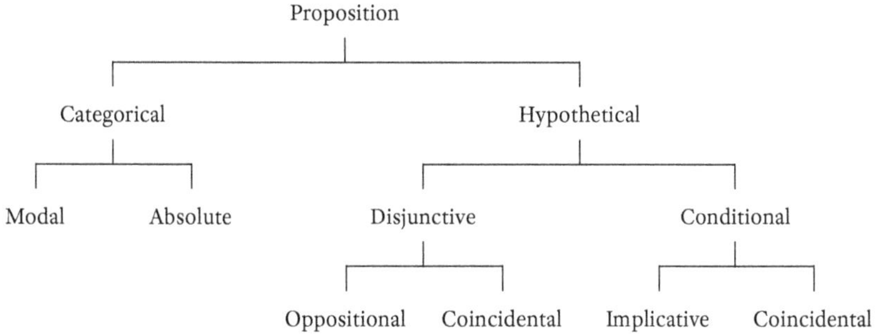

Figure 20: Relations among externalist and essentialist affirmatives (for §47)

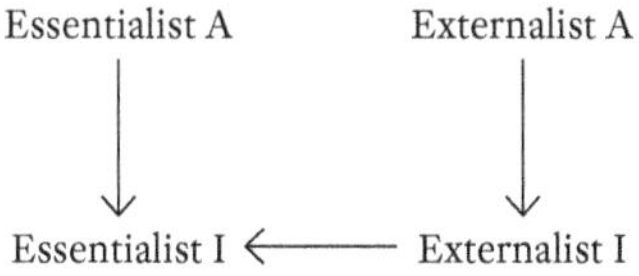

Figure 21: Relations among externalist and essentialist negatives (for §47)

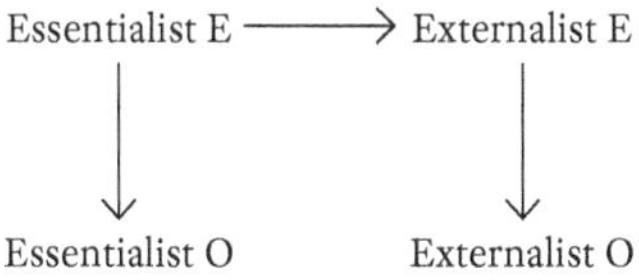

Figure 22: Implicational relations among simple propositions

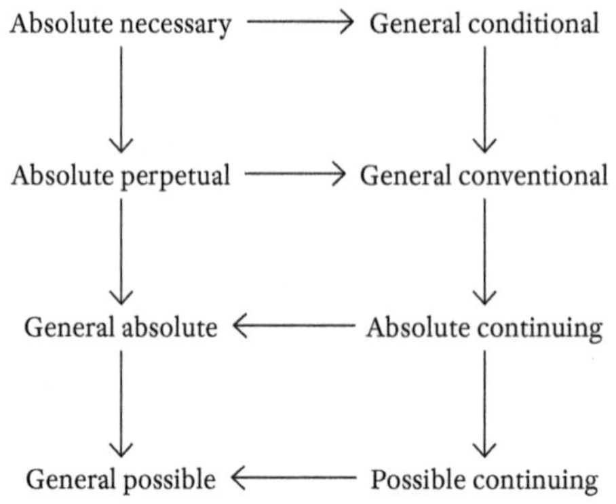

Figure 23: Implicational relations among subset of propositions first mentioned in §74

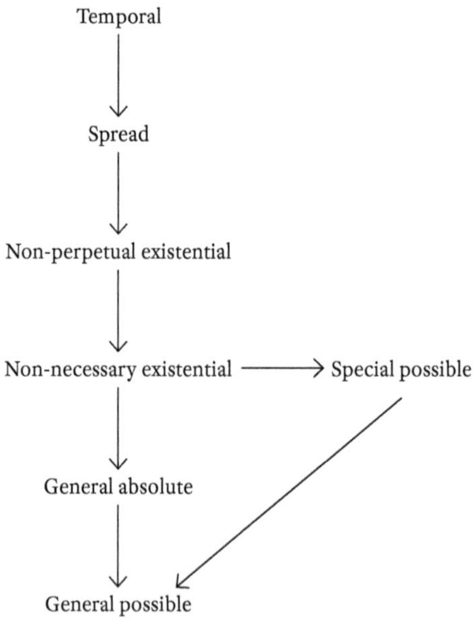

Figure 24: Square of opposition: referential necessity and possibility (for §69.1)

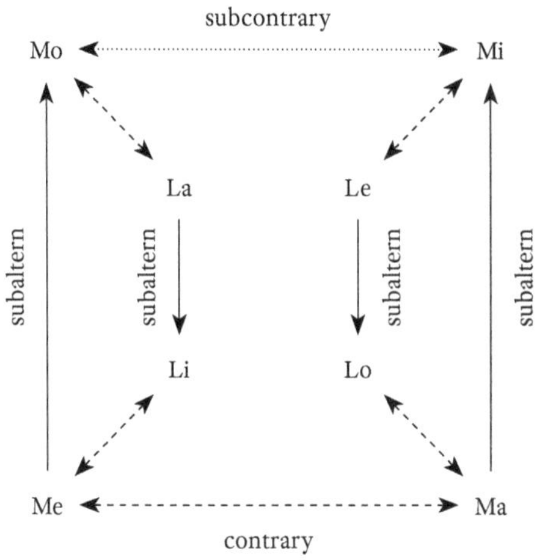

Figure 25: Square of opposition: descriptional necessity and possibility (for §69.4)

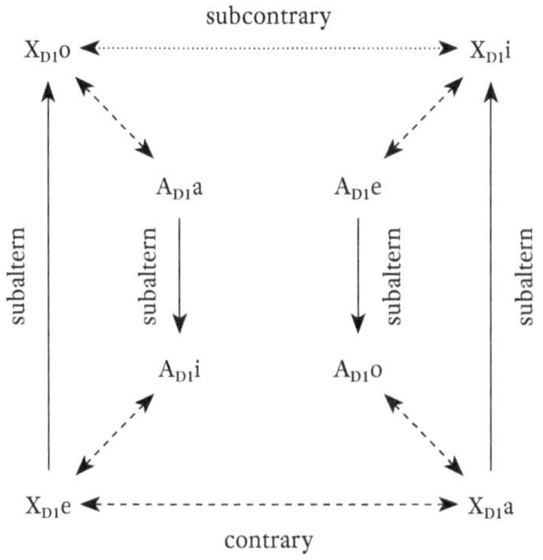

Figure 26: Referential L, A, X, and M: entailment and contradiction

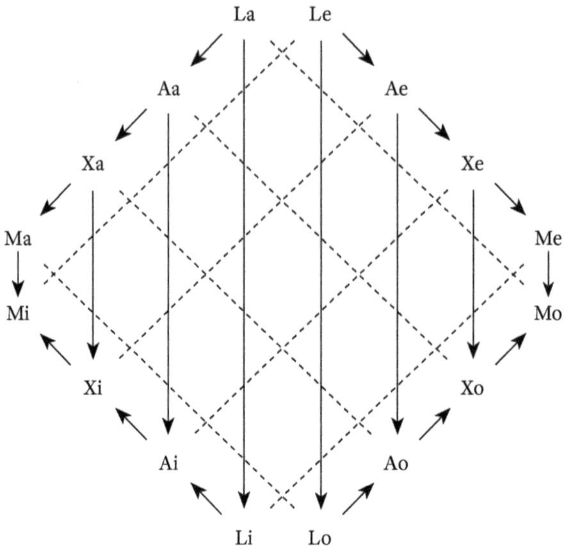

Figure 27: Descriptional L, A, X, and M: entailment and contradiction

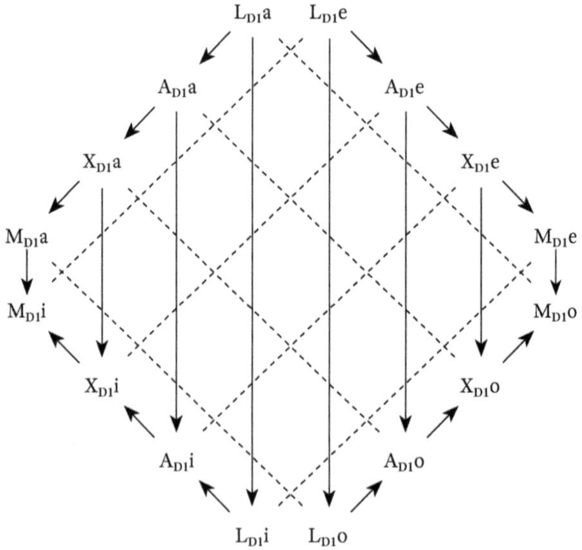

Figure 28: Square of opposition: conditionals (for §72)

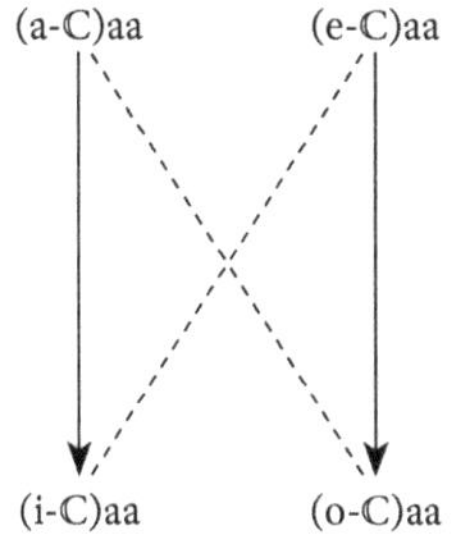

Figure 29: Implicational relations among hypothetical propositions claimed or implicit in §87.1

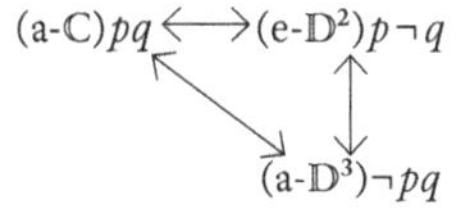

Figure 30: Conditionals entailed by exclusive disjunction as claimed in §87.2

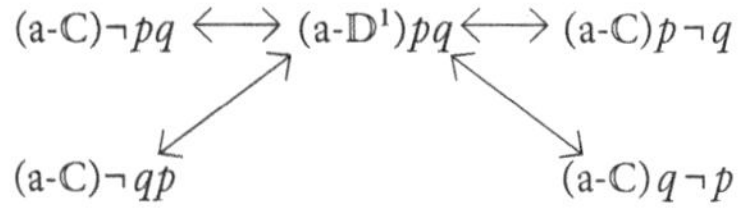

Figure 31: Mutual entailment between alternative denial ($\mathbb{D}^2$) and inclusive disjunction ($\mathbb{D}^3$) as claimed in §87.3

$$(\text{a-}\mathbb{D}^2)pq \longleftrightarrow (\text{e-}\mathbb{D}^3)\neg p \neg q$$

Figure 32: Al-Kātibī's primary division of the fallacies, *Jāmiʿ al-daqāʾiq*
(leaving aside fallacies from both fosrm and matter together)

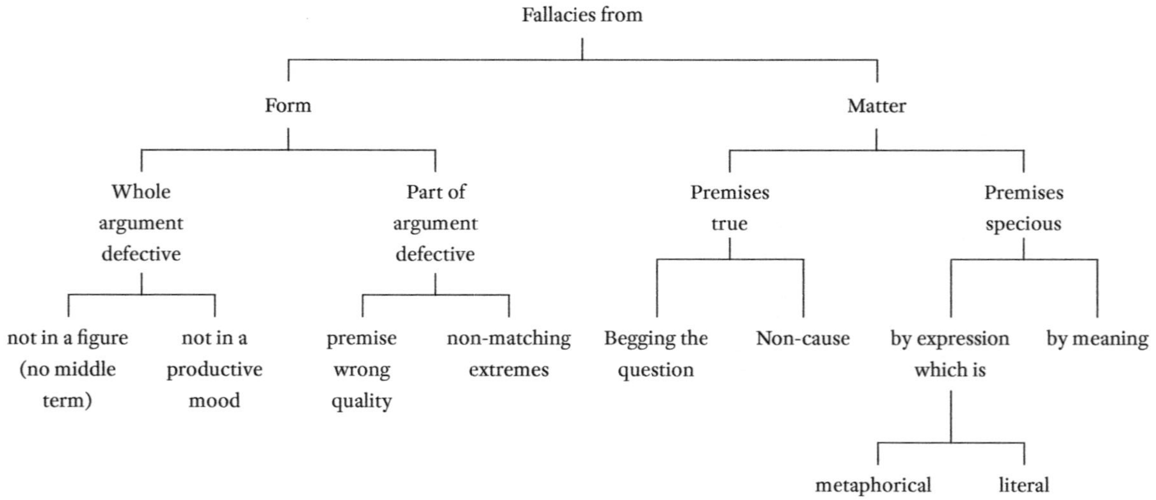

Appendix 1: Names of Propositions

I list here the translations of the names of the propositions as proposed by Rescher and Strobino, along with the symbols they use. I list the Rescher symbol and translation of the proposition's name, then Strobino's translation and symbol. I give my modification of the Strobino symbol in brackets at the end.

□E	absolute necessary (*ḍarūriyyah muṭlaqah*); referential necessity: **L**.
∀E	absolute perpetual (*dā'imah muṭlaqah*); referential perpetuity: **A**.
□C	general conditional (*mashrūṭah ʿāmmah*); descriptional unrestricted necessity: $\mathbf{L}_{D1}$.
∀C	general conventional (*ʿurfiyyah ʿāmmah*); descriptional unrestricted perpetuity: $\mathbf{A}_{D1}$.
∃E	general absolute (*muṭlaqah ʿāmmah*); referential one-sided absoluteness: $\mathbf{X}_1$.
◇E	general possibility (*mumkinah ʿāmmah*); referential one-sided possibility: $\mathbf{M}_1$.
□C&~∀E	special conditional (*mashrūṭah khāṣṣah*); descriptional restricted necessity: $\mathbf{L}_{D2}$.
∀C&~∀E	special conventional (*ʿurfiyyah khāṣṣah*); descriptional restricted perpetuity: $\mathbf{A}_{D2}$.
∃E&~□E	nonnecessary existential (*wujūdiyyah lā-ḍarūriyyah*); referential nonnecessary absoluteness: $\mathbf{X}_3$ ($\mathbf{X}_{\sim L}$).
∃E&~∀E	non-perpetual existential (*wujūdiyyah lā-dā'imah*); referential two-sided absoluteness: $\mathbf{X}_2$.
□T&~∀E	temporal (*waqtiyyah*); referential temporal determinate: **T** ($\mathbf{L}_{T2}$).
□S&~∀E	spread (*muntashirah*); referential temporal indeterminate: **U** ($\mathbf{L}_{X2}$).
◇E&~□E	special possibility (*mumkinah khāṣṣah*); referential two-sided possibility: $\mathbf{M}_2$.

Appendix 2: Propositional Forms

A: Every C is B (universal affirmative, *mūjibah kulliyyah*);
E: No C is B (universal negative, *sālibah kulliyyah*);
I: Some C is B (particular affirmative, *mūjibah juzʾiyyah*);
O: Some C is not B (particular negative, *sālibah juzʾiyyah*).

Modal propositions are given below in all four forms, first in Arabic with dummy variables (often there is no example in the *Rules*, and—caveat lector—I have set down what I believe would be al-Kātibī's phrasing), then in a close English translation, then in a translation in English that strikes me as natural, and that hopefully conveys the meaning of the proposition. I set out first the simple and then the compound propositions that are customarily investigated; I then go on to give only those further propositions that al-Kātibī refers to for the squares of opposition or in inferences.

The simple propositions customarily investigated

1. **L**: absolute necessity proposition (*ḍarūriyyah muṭlaqah*); referential necessity.

    L a-proposition: *bi-l-ḍarūrah kull jīm bāʾ*
    Necessarily, every C is B.
    Every C is necessarily B.

    L e-proposition: *bi-l-ḍarūrah lā shayʾ min jīm bāʾ*
    Necessarily, no C is B.
    No C is possibly B.

    L i-proposition: *bi-l-ḍarūrah baʿḍ jīm bāʾ*
    Necessarily, some C is B.
    Some C is necessarily B.

    L o-proposition: *bi-l-ḍarūrah baʿḍ jīm laysa bāʾ*
    Necessarily, some C is not B.
    Some C is not possibly B.

2. **A**: absolute perpetuity proposition (*dāʾimah muṭlaqah*); referential perpetuity.

   A a-proposition: *dāʾiman kull jīm bāʾ*
   Always, every C is B.
   Every C is always B.

   A e-proposition: *dāʾiman lā shayʾ min jīm bāʾ*
   Always, no C is B.
   No C is ever B.

   A i-proposition: *dāʾiman baʿḍ jīm bāʾ*
   Always, some C is B.
   Some C is always B.

   A o-proposition: *dāʾiman baʿḍ jīm laysa bāʾ*
   Always, some C is not B.
   Some C is never B.

3. $\mathbf{L_{D1}}$: general conditional (*mashrūṭah ʿāmmah*); descriptional unrestricted necessity.

   $\mathbf{L_{D1}}$ a-proposition: *bi-l-ḍarūrah kull jīm bāʾ mā dāma jīm*
   Necessarily, every C is B as long as it is C.
   Every C is necessarily B as long as it is C.

   $\mathbf{L_{D1}}$ e-proposition: *bi-l-ḍarūrah lā shayʾ min jīm bāʾ mā dāma jīm*
   Necessarily, no C is B as long as it is C.
   No C is possibly B as long as it is C.

   $\mathbf{L_{D1}}$ i-proposition: *bi-l-ḍarūrah baʿḍ jīm bāʾ mā dāma jīm*
   Necessarily, some C is B as long as it is C.
   Some C is necessarily B as long as it is C.

   $\mathbf{L_{D1}}$ o-proposition: *bi-l-ḍarūrah baʿḍ jīm laysa bāʾ mā dāma jīm*
   Necessarily, some C is not B as long as it is C.
   Some C is not possibly B as long as it is C.

4. $\mathbf{A_{D1}}$: general conventional (*ʿurfiyyah ʿāmmah*); descriptional unrestricted perpetuity.

$\mathbf{A_{D1}}$ a-proposition: *dāʾiman kull jīm bāʾ mā dāma jīm*
Always, every C is B as long as it is C.
Every C is always B as long as it is C.

$\mathbf{A_{D1}}$ e-proposition: *dāʾiman lā shayʾ min jīm bāʾ mā dāma jīm*
Always, no C is B as long as it is C.
No C is ever B as long as it is C.

$\mathbf{A_{D1}}$ i-proposition: *dāʾiman baʿḍ jīm bāʾ mā dāma jīm*
Always, some C is B as long as it is C.
Some C is always B as long as it is C.

$\mathbf{A_{D1}}$ o-proposition: *dāʾiman baʿḍ jīm laysa bāʾ mā dāma jīm*
Always, some C is not B as long as it is C.
Some C is not ever B as long as it is C.

5. $\mathbf{X_1}$: general absolute proposition (*muṭlaqah ʿāmmah*); referential one-sided absolute.

$\mathbf{X_1}$ a-proposition: *bi-l-iṭlāq al-ʿāmm kull jīm bāʾ*
By general absoluteness, every C is B.
Every C is at least once B.

$\mathbf{X_1}$ e-proposition: *bi-l-iṭlāq al-ʿāmm lā shayʾ min jīm bāʾ*
By general absoluteness, no C is B.
No C is always B.

$\mathbf{X_1}$ i-proposition: *bi-l-iṭlāq al-ʿāmm baʿḍ jīm bāʾ*
By general absoluteness, some C is B.
Some C is at least once B.

$\mathbf{X_1}$ o-proposition: *bi-l-iṭlāq al-ʿāmm baʿḍ jīm laysa bāʾ*
By general absoluteness, some C is not B.
Some C is not always B.

6. **M_1**: general possible proposition (*mumkinah ʿāmmah*); referential one-sided possibility.

 M_1 a-proposition: *bi-l-imkān al-ʿāmm kull jīm bāʾ*
 By general possibility, every C is B.
 Every C is possibly B.

 M_1 e-proposition: *bi-l-imkān al-ʿāmm lā shayʾ min jīm bāʾ*
 By general possibility, no C is B.
 No C is necessarily B.

 M_1 i-proposition: *bi-l-imkān al-ʿāmm baʿḍ jīm bāʾ*
 By general possibility, some C is B.
 Some C is possibly B.

 M_1 o-proposition: *bi-l-imkān al-ʿāmm baʿḍ jīm laysa bāʾ*
 By general possibility, some C is not B.
 Some C is not necessarily B.

The compound propositions customarily investigated

7. **L_{D2}**: special conditional (*mashrūṭah khāṣṣah*); descriptional restricted necessity.

 L_{D2} a-proposition: *bi-l-ḍarūrah kull jīm bāʾ mā dāma jīm lā dāʾiman*
 Necessarily, every C is B as long as it is C, not always.
 Every C is necessarily B as long as it is C, and no C is always B.

 L_{D2} e-proposition: *bi-l-ḍarūrah lā shayʾ min jīm bāʾ mā dāma jīm lā dāʾiman*
 Necessarily, no C is B as long as it is C, not always.
 No C is possibly B as long as it is C, and every C is at least once B.

 L_{D2} i-proposition: *bi-l-ḍarūrah baʿḍ jīm bāʾ mā dāma jīm lā dāʾiman*
 Necessarily, some C is B as long as it is C, not always.
 Some C is necessarily B as long as it is C, and those Cs are at least once not B.

L_{D2} o-proposition: *bi-l-ḍarūrah baʿḍ jīm laysa bāʾ mā dāma jīm lā dāʾiman*
Necessarily, some C is not B as long as it is C, not always.
Some C is not possibly B as long as it is C, and those Cs are at least once B.

8. **A_{D2}**: special conventional (*ʿurfiyyah khāṣṣah*); descriptional restricted perpetuity.

A_{D2} a-proposition: *dāʾiman kull jīm bāʾ mā dāma jīm lā dāʾiman*
Always, every C is B as long as it is C, not always.
Every C is always B as long as it is C, and no C is always B.

A_{D2} e-proposition: *dāʾiman lā shayʾ min jīm bāʾ mā dāma jīm lā dāʾiman*
Always, no C is B as long as it is C, not always.
No C is ever B as long as it is C, and every C is at least once B.

A_{D2} i-proposition: *dāʾiman baʿḍ jīm bāʾ mā dāma jīm lā dāʾiman*
Always, some C is B as long as it is C, not always.
Some C is always B as long as it is C, and those Cs are at least once not B.

A_{D2} o-proposition: *dāʾiman baʿḍ jīm laysa bāʾ mā dāma jīm lā dāʾiman*
Always, some C is not B as long as it is C, not always.
Some C is not ever B as long as it is C, and those Cs are at least once B.

9. **$X_{\sim L}$**: nonnecessary existential (*wujūdiyyah lā-ḍarūriyyah*); referential non-necessary absoluteness.

$X_{\sim L}$ a-proposition: *kull jīm bāʾ bi-l-fiʿl lā bi-l-ḍarūrah*
Actually, every C is B, not necessarily.
Every C is at least once B, and no C is necessarily B.

$X_{\sim L}$ e-proposition: *lā shayʾ min jīm bāʾ bi-l-fiʿl lā bi-l-ḍarūrah*
Actually, no C is B, not necessarily.
No C is always B, and every C is possibly B.

$X_{\sim L}$ i-proposition: *baʿḍ jīm bāʾ bi-l-fiʿl lā bi-l-ḍarūrah*
Actually, some C is B, not necessarily.
Some C is at least once B, and those Cs are possibly not B.

$X_{\sim L}$ o-proposition: *baʿḍ jīm laysa bāʾ bi-l-fiʿl lā bi-l-ḍarūrah*
Actually, some C is not B, not necessarily.
Some C is not always B, and those Cs are possibly B.

10. **X_2**: non-perpetual existential (*wujūdiyyah lā-dāʾimah*); referential two-sided absoluteness.

X_2 a-proposition: *kull jīm bāʾ bi-l-fiʿl lā dāʾiman*
Actually, every C is B, not always.
Every C is at least once B, and no C is always B.

X_2 e-proposition: *lā shayʾ min jīm bāʾ bi-l-fiʿl lā dāʾiman*
Actually, no C is B, not always.
No C is always B, and every C is at least once B.

X_2 i-proposition: *baʿḍ jīm bāʾ bi-l-fiʿl lā dāʾiman*
Actually, some C is B, not always.
Some C is at least once B, and those Cs are not always B.

X_2 o-proposition: *baʿḍ jīm laysa bāʾ bi-l-fiʿl lā dāʾiman*
Actually, some C is not B, not always.
Some C is not always B, and those Cs are at least once B.

11. **L_{T2}**: temporal (*waqtiyyah*); referential temporal determinate.

See Appendix 4.

L_{T2} a-proposition: *bi-l-ḍarūrah kull qamar munkhasif waqt ḥaylūlat al-arḍ baynahu wa-bayna l-shams lā dāʾiman*
Necessarily, every moon is eclipsed on the earth's coming between it and the sun, not always.
Necessarily, every C is B at time T, not always.
Every C is necessarily B at time T, and no C is always B.

L_{T2} e-proposition: *bi-l-ḍarūrah lā shayʾ min al-qamar bi-munkhasif waqt al-tarbīʿ lā dāʾiman*
Necessarily, no moon is eclipsed at the moment of quadrature, not always.
Necessarily, no C is B at time T, not always.
No C is possibly B at time T, and every C is at least once B.

L_{T2} i-proposition: *bi-l-ḍarūrah baʿḍ qamar munkhasif waqt ḥaylūlat al-arḍ baynahu wa-bayna l-shams lā dāʾiman*
Necessarily, some moon is eclipsed on the earth's coming between it and the sun, not always.
Necessarily, some C is B at time T, not always.
Some C is necessarily B at time T, and those Cs are not always B.

L_{T2} o-proposition: *bi-l-ḍarūrah baʿḍ qamar laysa bi-munkhasif waqt al-tarbīʿ lā dāʾiman*
Necessarily, some moon is not eclipsed at the moment of quadrature, not always.
Necessarily, some C is not B at time T, not always.
Some C is not possibly B at time T, and those Cs are at least once B.

12. **L_{X2}**: spread (*muntashirah*); referential temporal indeterminate.

See Appendix 4.

L_{X2} a-proposition: *bi-l-ḍarūrah kull insān mutanaffis fī waqt mā lā dāʾiman*
Necessarily, every man breathes at a given time, not always.
Necessarily, every C is B at some time, not always.
Every C is necessarily B at some time, and no C is always B.

L_{X2} e-proposition: *bi-l-ḍarūrah lā shayʾ min al-insān bi-mutanaffis fī waqt mā lā dāʾiman*
Necessarily, no man breathes at a given time, not always.
Necessarily, no C is B at some time, not always.
No C is possibly B at some time, and every C is at least once B.

L_{X2} i-proposition: *bi-l-ḍarūrah baʿḍ jīm bāʾ fī waqt mā lā dāʾiman*
Necessarily, some C is B at some time, not always.
Some C is necessarily B at some time, and those Cs are not always B.

L_{X2} o-proposition: *bi-l-ḍarūrah baʿḍ jīm laysa bāʾ fī waqt mā lā dāʾiman*
Necessarily, some C is not B at some time, not always.
Some C is not possibly B at some time, and those Cs are at least once B.

13. **M_2**: special possible (*mumkinah khāṣṣah*); referential two-sided possibility.

M_2 a-proposition: *kull jīm bāʾ bi-l-imkān lā bi-l-ḍarūrah*
Possibly, every C is B, not necessarily.
Every C is possibly B, and no C is necessarily B.

M_2 e-proposition: *lā shayʾ min jīm bāʾ bi-l-imkān lā bi-l-ḍarūrah*
Possibly, no C is B, not necessarily.
No C is necessarily B, and every C is possibly B.

M_2 i-proposition: *baʿḍ jīm bāʾ bi-l-imkān lā bi-l-ḍarūrah*
Possibly, some C is B, not necessarily.
Some C is possibly B, and those Cs are not necessarily B.

M_2 o-proposition: *baʿḍ jīm laysa bāʾ bi-l-imkān lā bi-l-ḍarūrah*
Possibly, some C is not B, not necessarily.
Some C is not necessarily B, and those Cs are possibly B.

Unlisted simple propositions called on by al-Kātibī

14. **L_{T1}**: absolute temporal (*al-waqtiyyah al-muṭlaqah*); assumed in working out the contradictories for **L_{T2}** as one of its component propositions; conclusion to some first-figure syllogistic mixes; see Appendix 4.

L_{T1} a-proposition: *kull jīm bāʾ bi-l-ḍarūrah fī waqt muʿayyan*
Necessarily, every C is B at time T.
Every C is necessarily B at time T.

L_{T1} e-proposition: *lā shayʾ min jīm bāʾ bi-l-ḍarūrah fī waqt muʿayyan*
Necessarily, no C is B at time T.
No C is possibly B at time T.

L_{T1} i-proposition: *baʿḍ jīm bāʾ bi-l-ḍarūrah fī waqt muʿayyan*
Necessarily, some C is B at time T.
Some C is necessarily B at time T.

L_{T1} o-proposition: *baʿḍ jīm laysa bāʾ bi-l-ḍarūrah fī waqt muʿayyan*
Necessarily, some C is not B at time T.
Some C is not possibly B at time T.

15. $\mathbf{L}_{X1}$: absolute spread (*al-muntashirah al-muṭlaqah*); assumed in working out the contradictories for $\mathbf{L}_{X2}$ as one of its component propositions; conclusion to some first-figure syllogistic mixes.

    $\mathbf{L}_{X1}$ a-proposition: *kull jīm bāʾ bi-l-ḍarūrah fī waqt mā*
    Necessarily, every C is B at some time.
    Every C is necessarily B at some time.

    $\mathbf{L}_{X1}$ e-proposition: *lā shayʾ min jīm bāʾ bi-l-ḍarūrah fī waqt mā*
    Necessarily, no C is B at time T.
    No C is possibly B at time T.

    $\mathbf{L}_{X1}$ i-proposition: *baʿḍ jīm bāʾ bi-l-ḍarūrah fī waqt mā*
    Necessarily, some C is B at some time.
    Some C is necessarily B at some time.

    $\mathbf{L}_{X1}$ o-proposition: *baʿḍ jīm laysa bāʾ bi-l-ḍarūrah fī waqt mā*
    Necessarily, some C is not B at some time.
    Some C is not possibly B at some time.

16. $\mathbf{X}_{T1}$: temporal absolute (*al-muṭlaqah al-waqtiyyah*); conclusion in some first- and second-figure mixes.

    I don't think I've ever seen $\mathbf{X}_{T1}$ written out as a proposition in full, whether with dummy letters or concrete terms; see $\mathbf{M}_{T1}$ in Appendix 4.

    $\mathbf{X}_{T1}$ a-proposition: *kull jīm bāʾ bi-l-fiʿl fī waqt muʿayyan*
    By general absoluteness, every C is B at time T.
    Every C is actually B at time T.

    $\mathbf{X}_{T1}$ e-proposition: *lā shayʾ min jīm bāʾ bi-l-fiʿl fī waqt muʿayyan*
    By general absoluteness, no C is B at time T.
    No C is actually B at time T.

    $\mathbf{X}_{T1}$ i-proposition: *baʿḍ jīm bāʾ bi-l-fiʿl fī waqt muʿayyan*
    By general absoluteness, some C is B at time T.
    Some C is actually B at time T.

    $\mathbf{X}_{T1}$ o-proposition: *baʿḍ jīm laysa bāʾ bi-l-fiʿl fī waqt muʿayyan*
    By general absoluteness, some C is not B at time T.
    Some C is not actually B at time T.

17. $\mathbf{X}_{X1}$: spread absolute (*al-muṭlaqah al-muntashirah*); again, a conclusion in some first- and second-figure mixes.

I don't think I've ever seen $\mathbf{X}_{X1}$ written out as a proposition in full, whether with dummy letters or concrete terms; this is my best guess.

$\mathbf{X}_{X1}$ a-proposition: *kull jīm bāʾ bi-l-fiʿl fī waqt mā*
By general absoluteness, every C is B at some time.
Every C is actually B at some time.

$\mathbf{X}_{X1}$ e-proposition: *lā shayʾ min jīm bāʾ bi-l-fiʿl fī waqt mā*
By general absoluteness, no C is B at some time.
No C is actually B at some time.

$\mathbf{X}_{X1}$ i-proposition: *baʿḍ jīm bāʾ bi-l-fiʿl fī waqt mā*
By general absoluteness, some C is B at some time.
Some C is actually B at some time.

$\mathbf{X}_{X1}$ o-proposition: *baʿḍ jīm laysa bāʾ bi-l-fiʿl fī waqt mā*
By general absoluteness, some C is not B at some time.
Some C is not actually B at some time.

18. $\mathbf{M}_{T1}$: temporal possible (*al-mumkinah al-waqtiyyah*); given as contradictory of $\mathbf{L}_{T1}$, a component of $\mathbf{L}_{T2}$.

See Appendix 4, though note al-Ḥillī gives *fī dhālika l-waqt* for *fī waqt muʿayyan.*

$\mathbf{M}_{T1}$ a-proposition: *kull jīm bāʾ bi-l-imkān fī waqt muʿayyan*
Possibly, every C is B at time T.
Every C is possibly B at time T.

$\mathbf{M}_{T1}$ e-proposition: *lā shayʾ min jīm bāʾ bi-l-imkān fī waqt muʿayyan*
Possibly, no C is B at time T.
No C is necessarily B at time T.

$\mathbf{M}_{T1}$ i-proposition: *baʿḍ jīm bāʾ bi-l-imkān fī waqt muʿayyan*
Possibly, some C is B at time T.
Some C is possibly B at time T.

M_{T1} o-proposition: *baʿḍ jīm laysa bāʾ bi-l-imkān fī waqt muʿayyan*
Possibly, some C is not B at time T.
Some C is not necessarily B at time T.

19. **M_A**: perpetual possible (*al-mumkinah al-dāʾimah*); given as contradictory of **L_{X1}**, a component of **L_{X2}**.

See Appendix 4; I adopt the name for this proposition given by al-Khūnajī, *Kashf al-asrār*, 126.11, and Rescher and vander Nat, "Theory of Modal Syllogistic," 25.

M_A a-proposition: *kull jīm bāʾ bi-l-imkān dāʾiman*
Always, every C is possibly B.

M_A e-proposition: *lā shayʾ min jīm bāʾ bi-l-imkān dāʾiman*
Always, no C is necessarily B.

M_A i-proposition: *baʿḍ jīm bāʾ bi-l-imkān dāʾiman*
Always, some C is possibly B.

M_A o-proposition: *baʿḍ jīm laysa bāʾ bi-l-imkān dāʾiman*
Always, some C is not necessarily B.

20. **X_{D1}**: absolute continuing (*al-ḥīniyyah al-muṭlaqah*); given as contradictory of **A_{D1}**, and as conclusion to a number of third- and fourth-figure syllogistic mixes.

The *ḥīna*-clause is given in some examples as *fī baʿḍ awqāt kawnihi jīm*, for example in §69.3: "Everyone afflicted with pleurisy may cough at times while afflicted" (*kull man bi-hi dhāt al-janb yumkinu an yasʿala fī baʿḍ awqāt kawnihi majnūban*). *Bi-l-iṭlāq al-ʿāmm* could be put at the beginning or end of the proposition.

X_{D1} a-proposition: *kull jīm bāʾ ḥīna huwa jīm*
Every C is [at least once] B while it is C.
Every C is at least once B while C.

X_{D1} e-proposition: *lā shayʾ min jīm bāʾ ḥīna huwa jīm*
No C is [always] B while it is C.
No C is always B while C.

X_{D1} i-proposition: *baʿḍ jīm bāʾ ḥīna huwa jīm*
Some C is [at least once] B while it is C.
Some C is at least once B while C.

X_{D1} o-proposition: *baʿḍ jīm laysa bāʾ ḥīna huwa jīm*
Some C is not B [at least once] while it is C.
Some C is not always B while C.

21. **M_{D1}**: possible continuing (*al-ḥīniyyah al-mumkinah*); given as contradictory of **L_{D1}**.

As with **X_{D1}**. The *ḥīna*-clause can be replaced with *fī baʿḍ awqāt kawnihi jīm*; *bi-l-imkān al-ʿāmm* can be replaced as in the example given for 20, which is to say, by the modalized copula, *yumkinu an yakūna*.

M_{D1} a-proposition: *bi-l-imkān al-ʿāmm kull jīm bāʾ ḥīna huwa jīm*
Possibly, every C is B while C.
Every C is possibly B while C.

M_{D1} e-proposition: *bi-l-imkān al-ʿāmm lā shayʾ min jīm bāʾ ḥīna huwa jīm*
Possibly, no C is B while C.
No C is necessarily B while C.

M_{D1} i-proposition: *bi-l-imkān al-ʿāmm baʿḍ jīm bāʾ ḥīna huwa jīm*
Possibly, some C is B while C.
Some C is possibly B while C.

M_{D1} o-proposition: *bi-l-imkān al-ʿāmm baʿḍ jīm laysa bāʾ ḥīna huwa jīm*
Possibly, some C is not B while C.
Some C is not necessarily B while C.

Unlisted compound propositions called on by al-Kātibī

Al-Kātibī mentions six more compound propositions as conclusions to inferences.

22. **L_2**: non-perpetual necessary (impossible proposition) (*al-ḍarūriyyah al-lā-dā'imah*), given as conclusion to a first-figure mix.

    L_2 a-proposition: *bi-l-ḍarūrah kull jīm bā' lā dā'iman*
    Every C is necessarily B, not always.
    Every C is necessarily B, and no C is always B.

    L_2 e-proposition: *bi-l-ḍarūrah lā shay' min jīm bā' lā dā'iman*
    Necessarily, no C is B, not always.
    No C is possibly B, and every C is at least once B.

    L_2 i-proposition: *bi-l-ḍarūrah baʿḍ jīm bā' lā dā'iman*
    Necessarily, some C is B, not always.
    Some Cs are necessarily B, and those Cs are at least once not B.

    L_2 o-proposition: *bi-l-ḍarūrah baʿḍ jīm laysa bā' lā dā'iman*
    Necessarily, some C is not B, not always.
    Some Cs are not possibly B, and those Cs are at least once B.

23. **A_2**: non-perpetual perpetual (impossible proposition) (*al-dā'imah al-lā-dā'imah*), given as conclusion to some first-figure mixes.

    A_2 a-proposition: *dā'iman kull jīm bā' lā dā'iman*
    Always, every C is B, not always.
    Every C is always B, and no C is always B.

    A_2 e-proposition: *dā'iman lā shay' min jīm bā' lā dā'iman*
    Always, no C is B, not always.
    No C is ever B, and every C is at least once B.

    A_2 i-proposition: *dā'iman baʿḍ jīm bā' lā dā'iman*
    Always, some C is B, not always.
    Some Cs are always B, and those Cs are at least once not B.

    A_2 o-proposition: *dā'iman baʿḍ jīm laysa bā' lā dā'iman*
    Always, some C is not B, not always.
    Some Cs are not ever B, and those Cs are at least once B.

24. **$A_{D(2)}$**: non-perpetual-for-some conventional (*al-ʿurfiyyah lā dāʾimah li-l-baʿḍ*), given as converse of certain propositions, and as conclusion for some fourth-figure mixes.

$A_{D(2)}$ a-proposition: *dāʾiman kull jīm bāʾ mā dāma jīm lā dāʾiman li-l-baʿḍ*
Always, every C is B as long as it is C, not always for some.
Every C is always B as long as it is C, and some C is not always B.

A_{D2} e-proposition: *dāʾiman lā shayʾ min jīm bāʾ mā dāma jīm lā dāʾiman li-l-baʿḍ*
Always, no C is B as long as it is C, not always for some.
No C is ever B as long as it is C, and some C is at least once B.

A_{D2} i-proposition: *dāʾiman baʿḍ jīm bāʾ mā dāma jīm lā dāʾiman li-l-baʿḍ*
Always, some C is B as long as it is C, not always for some.
Some C is always B as long as it is C, and some of those Cs are not always B.

A_{D2} o-proposition: *dāʾiman baʿḍ jīm laysa bāʾ mā dāma jīm lā dāʾiman li-l-baʿḍ*
Always, some C is not B as long as it is C, not always for some.
Some C is not ever B as long as it is C, and some of those Cs are at least once B.

25. **X_{T2}**: non-perpetual temporal absolute (*al-muṭlaqah al-waqtiyyah al-lā-dāʾimah*); conclusion for a first-figure mix.

X_{T2} a-proposition: *kull jīm bāʾ fī waqt muʿayyan lā dāʾiman*
Every C is B at time T, not always.
Every C is B at time T, and no C is always B.

X_{T2} e-proposition: *lā shayʾ min jīm bāʾ fī waqt muʿayyan lā dāʾiman*
No C is B at time T, not always.
No C is B at time T, and every C is at least once B.

X_{T2} i-proposition: *baʿḍ jīm bāʾ fī waqt muʿayyan lā dāʾiman*
Some C is B at time T, not always.
Some C is B at time T, and those Cs are not always B.

$\mathbf{X}_{T2}$ o-proposition: *baʿḍ jīm laysa bāʾ fī waqt muʿayyan lā dāʾiman*
Some C is not B at time T, not always.
Some C is not B at time T, and those Cs are at least once B.

26. $\mathbf{X}_{X2}$: non-perpetual spread absolute (*al-muṭlaqah al-muntashirah al-lā-dāʾimah*); conclusion for a first-figure mix.

$\mathbf{X}_{X2}$ a-proposition: *kull jīm bāʾ fī waqt mā lā dāʾiman*
Every C is B at some time, not always.
Every C is B at some time, and no C is always B.

$\mathbf{X}_{X2}$ e-proposition: *lā shayʾ min jīm bāʾ fī waqt mā lā dāʾiman*
No C is B at some time, not always.
No C is B at some time, and every C is at least once B.

$\mathbf{X}_{X2}$ i-proposition: *baʿḍ jīm bāʾ fī waqt mā lā dāʾiman*
Some C is B at some time, not always.
Some C is B at some time, and those Cs are not always B.

$\mathbf{X}_{X2}$ o-proposition: *baʿḍ jīm laysa bāʾ fī waqt mā lā dāʾiman*
Some C is not B at some time, not always.
Some C is not B at some time, and those Cs are at least once B.

27. $\mathbf{X}_{D2}$: non-perpetual absolute continuing (*al-ḥīniyyah al-muṭlaqah al-lā-dāʾimah*)

$\mathbf{X}_{D2}$ a-proposition: *kull jīm bāʾ ḥīna huwa jīm lā dāʾiman*
Every C is [at least once] B while it is C, not always.
Every C is at least once B while C, and no C is always B.

$\mathbf{X}_{D2}$ e-proposition: *lā shayʾ min jīm bāʾ ḥīna huwa jīm lā dāʾiman*
No C is [always] B while it is C, not always.
No C is always B while C, and every C is at least once B.

$\mathbf{X}_{D2}$ i-proposition: *baʿḍ jīm bāʾ ḥīna huwa jīm lā dāʾiman*
Some C is [at least once] B while it is C, not always.
Some C is at least once B while C, and those Cs are not always B.

$\mathbf{X}_{D2}$ o-proposition: *baʿḍ jīm laysa bāʾ ḥīna huwa jīm lā dāʾiman*
Some C is not B [at least once] while it is C, not always.
Some C is not always B while C, and those Cs are at least once B.

Appendix 3: Examples of Quantified Hypothetical Propositions

The following examples are taken from al-Ḥillī, *al-Qawāʿid al-jaliyyah*, 285–86.

Conditionals:

A-conditional: (a-ℂ)aa. Whenever the sun is up, then it is day (*kullamā kānat al-shams ṭāliʿah fa-l-nahār mawjūd*; alternatives to *kullamā*: *mahmā*, *matā*);

E-conditional: (e-ℂ)aa. Never, if the sun is up, then it is night (*laysa al-battata idhā kānat al-shams ṭāliʿah fa-l-layl mawjūd*);

I-conditional: (i-ℂ)aa. Sometimes, if the sun is up, then it is day (*qad yakūnu idhā kānat al-shams ṭāliʿah fa-l-nahār mawjūd*);

O-proposition: (o-ℂ)aa. Two forms (no examples given): (1) Sometimes not, if P then Q (*qad lā yakūnu*); (2) Not always, if P then Q (*laysa kullamā*, or *laysa mahmā*, or *laysa matā*).

Disjunctives:

A-proposition: (a-𝔻)aa. Always, either the sun is up, or it is not (*dāʾiman immā an takūna l-shams ṭāliʿah aw lā takūna*);

E-proposition: (e-𝔻)aa. Never, either the sun is up, or it is day (*laysa al-battata immā an takūna l-shams ṭāliʿah wa-immā an yakūna l-nahār mawjūdan*);

I-proposition: (i-𝔻)aa. Sometimes, either the sun is up, or it is night (*qad yakūnu immā an takūna l-shams ṭāliʿah wa-immā an yakūna l-layl mawjūdan*);

O-proposition: (o-𝔻)aa. Two forms (no examples given): (1) Sometimes not, either P or Q (*qad lā yakūnu*); (2) Not always, either P or Q (*laysa dāʾiman*).

Appendix 4: Contradictories for Modalized Propositions

Here is a summary of the a- and o-proposition contradictories:

L/M The absolute necessity proposition has as its contradictory the general possibility proposition: "every A is necessarily B" contradicts "some A is not necessarily B" (or "some A is possibly not B").

A/X The absolute perpetual has the general absolute: "every A is always B" contradicts "some A is not always B" (or "some A is sometimes not B").

L_{D1}/M_{D1} The general conditional has the continuing possibility (*ḥīniyyah mumkinah*): "every A is necessarily B as long as it is A" contradicts "some A is possibly not B while A" (or "some A is not necessarily B while A").

A_{D1}/X_{D1} The general conventional has the continuing absolute (*ḥīniyyah muṭlaqah*): "every A is always B as long as it is A" contradicts "some A is sometimes not B while A" (or "some A is not always B while A").

Compounds (read subject to §71; taken from al-Ḥillī, *al-Qawāʿid al-jaliyyah*, 295–96):

L_{D2} a-proposition contradicts **M_{D1}** o-proposition or **A** i-proposition: the contradictory of "every C is necessarily B as long as it is C, not always" is "either some C is not necessarily B while C, or some C is always B" (*naqīḍ kull jīm bi-l-ḍarūrah bāʾ mā dāma jīm lā dāʾiman immā baʿḍ jīm laysa bāʾ bi-l-imkān ḥīna huwa jīm aw baʿḍ jīm bāʾ dāʾiman*);

A_{D2} a-proposition contradicts **X_{D1}** o-proposition or **A** i-proposition: the contradictory of "every C is always B as long as it is C, not always" is "either some C is not always B while C, or some C is always B" (*naqīḍ kull jīm bāʾ mā dāma jīm lā dāʾiman immā baʿḍ jīm laysa bāʾ ḥīna huwa jīm aw baʿḍ jīm bāʾ dāʾiman*);

X_2 a-proposition contradicts **A** i-proposition or **A** o-proposition: the contradictory of "every C is B, not always" is "either some C is always B, or some C is never B" (*naqīḍ kull jīm bāʾ lā dāʾiman immā baʿḍ jīm bāʾ dāʾiman aw baʿḍ jīm laysa bāʾ dāʾiman*);

X$_{\sim L}$ a-proposition contradicts **A** o-proposition or **L** i-proposition: the contradictory of "every C is B, not necessarily" is "either some C is never B, or some C is necessarily B" (*naqīḍ kullu jīm bāʾ lā bi-l-ḍarūrah immā baʿḍ jīm laysa bāʾ dāʾiman aw baʿḍ jīm bāʾ bi-l-ḍarūrah*);

L$_{T2}$ a-proposition contradicts **M**$_{T}$ o-proposition or **A** i-proposition: the temporal is a compound of an absolute temporal (*waqtiyyah muṭlaqah*) and a general absolute, so its contradictory is either a possibility temporal or a perpetuity; so the contradictory of "every C is B necessarily at a specified time, not always" is "either possibly at that time some C is not B, or some C is always B" (*naqīḍ kull jīm bāʾ lā bi-l-ḍarūrah fī waqt muʿayyan lā dāʾiman immā baʿḍ jīm laysa bāʾ bi-l-imkān fī dhālika l-waqt aw baʿḍ jīm bāʾ dāʾiman*);

L$_{X2}$ a-proposition contradicts **M**$_{A}$ o-proposition or **A** i-proposition: the spread is a compound of an absolute spread (*muntashirah muṭlaqah*) and a general absolute, so its contradictory is either a perpetual possible or a perpetual; so the contradictory of "every C is B necessarily at some time, not always" is "either always some C is not necessarily B, or some C is always B" (*naqīḍ kull jīm bāʾ lā bi-l-ḍarūrah fī waqt mā lā dāʾiman immā baʿḍ jīm laysa bāʾ bi-l-imkān dāʾiman aw baʿḍ jīm bāʾ dāʾiman*);

M$_{2}$ a-proposition contradicts **L** o-proposition or **L** i-proposition: the contradictory of "every C is B by a special possibility" is "either some C is not possibly B or some C is necessarily B" (*naqīḍ kull jīm bāʾ bi-l-imkān al-khāṣṣ immā baʿḍ jīm laysa bāʾ bi-l-ḍarūrah aw baʿḍ jīm bāʾ bi-l-ḍarūrah*).

Bibliography

Ahmed, Asad Q., trans. *Avicenna's Deliverance: Logic*. Karachi: Oxford University Press, 2011.

Aristotle. *Manṭiq Arisṭū*. Edited by ʿAbd al-Raḥmān Badawī. 2 vols. Cairo: Maṭbaʿat Dār al-Kutub al-Miṣriyyah, 1948.

Averroes. *Le philosophe et la loi: Édition, traduction et commentaire de l'abrégé du Mustaṣfā*. Edited, translated, and commented by Ziad Bou Akl. Scientia Graeco-Arabica, vol. 14. Berlin: De Gruyter, 2015.

Avicenna. *Fontes Sapientiae* (*ʿUyūn al-ḥikmah*). Edited by ʿAbdurraḥmān Badawi. Cairo: Publications de l'Institut Français d'Archéologie Orientale du Caire, 1954.

———. *Kitāb al-Ishārāt wa-l-tanbīhāt: Le livre des théorèmes et des avertissements*. Vol. 1. Translated by J. Forget. Leiden, Netherlands: Brill, 1892.

———. *Manṭiq al-mashriqiyyīn (Oriental Logic)*. Edited by M. D. al-Khaṭīb and ʿA. F. al-Qatlān. Cairo: al-Maktabah al-Salafiyyah, 1910.

———. *The Metaphysics of The Healing: A Parallel English–Arabic Text*. Translated by Michael E. Marmura. Provo, Utah: Brigham Young University Press, 2005.

———. *Al-Najāt min al-gharaq fī baḥr al-ḍalālāt*. Edited by M. Dānishpazhūh. Tehran: Enteshārāt-e Dāneshgāh, 1985.

———. *Al-Shifāʾ: al-Ilāhiyyāt*. *See* Avicenna, *The Metaphysics of the Healing*.

———. *Al-Shifāʾ: al-Manṭiq: al-Burhān*. Edited by A. A. ʿAfīfī. Cairo: al-Maṭbaʿah al-Amīrīyah, 1956.

———. *Al-Shifāʾ: al-Manṭiq: al-ʿIbārah*. Edited by M. M. al-Khuḍayrī. Cairo: al-Hayʾah al-Miṣrīyyah al-ʿĀmmah li-l-Taʾlīf wa-l-Nashr, 1970.

———. *Al-Shifāʾ: al-Manṭiq: al-Madkhal*. *See* Di Vincenzo, *Avicenna, The Healing, Logic: Isagoge*.

———. *Al-Shifāʾ: al-Manṭiq: al-Maqūlāt*. Edited by I. Madkour, A. Ahwānī, G. Anawati, M. M. al-Khuḍayrī, and S. Zāyid. Cairo: al-Hayʾah al-ʿĀmmah li-Shuʾūn al-Maṭābiʿ al-Amīriyyah, 1959.

———. *Al-Shifāʾ: al-Manṭiq: al-Qiyās*. Edited by S. Zāyid. Cairo: al-Hayʾah al-ʿĀmmah li-Shuʾūn al-Maṭābiʿ al-Amīriyyah, 1964.

Al-Baghdādī, Abū l-Barakāt. *Al-Kitāb al-muʿtabar fī l-ḥikmah.* Edited by Zayn al-ʿĀbidīn al-Mūsawī, ʿAbdallāh ibn Aḥmad al-ʿAlawī, Aḥmad ibn Muḥammad al-Yamānī, and Muḥammad ʿĀdil al-Quddīsī. Hyderabad, India: Jamʿiyyat Dāʾirat al-Maʿārif al-ʿUthmāniyyah, 1939.

Barhebraeus. *Specimen Historiae Arabum, Sive, Gregorii Abul Farajii Malatiensis de Origine & Moribus Arabum Succincta Narratio, in Linguam Latinam Conversa, Notisque e Probatissimis apud Ipsos Authoribus, Fusius Illustrata.* Translated by Edward Pococke. Oxford: H. Hall, 1663.

Barnes, Jonathan. *Porphyry: Introduction.* New York: Oxford University Press, 2003.

Al-Bayḍāwī, ʿAbdallāh. *Nature, Man and God in Medieval Islam: ʿAbd Allah Baydawi's Text, Tawaliʿ al-Anwar min Mataliʿ al-Anzar, along with Mahmud Isfahani's Commentary, Mataliʿ al-Anzar, Sharh Tawaliʿ al-Anwar.* Islamic Philosophy, Theology and Science. Texts and Studies, vol. 47. Edited and translated by Edwin E. Calverley and James W. Pollock. Leiden, Netherlands: Brill, 2002.

Benevich, Fedor. "Scepticism and Semantics in Twelfth-Century Arabic Philosophy." *Theoria* 88 (2022): 72–108.

Black, Deborah L. *Logic and Aristotle's Rhetoric and Poetics in Medieval Arabic Philosophy.* Islamic Philosophy, Theology and Science. Texts and Studies, vol. 7. Leiden, Netherlands: Brill, 1990.

Buridan, John. *Summulae de Dialectica. See* Klima, *John Buridan, Summulae de Dialectica.*

Copenhaver, Brian P., Calvin G. Normore, and Terence Parsons, trans. *Peter of Spain: Summaries of Logic; Text, Translation, Introduction, and Notes.* Oxford: Oxford University Press, 2014.

Davidson, Herbert A. *Alfarabi, Avicenna, and Averroes on Intellect: Their Cosmologies, Theories of the Active Intellect, and Theories of Human Intellect.* New York: Oxford University Press, 1992.

Di Vincenzo, Silvia. *Avicenna, The Healing, Logic: Isagoge: A New Edition, English Translation and Commentary of the Kitāb al-Madḫal of Avicenna's Kitāb al-Šifāʾ.* Scientia Graeco-Arabica, vol. 31. Berlin: De Gruyter, 2021.

Eichner, Heidrun. "The Post-Avicennian Philosophical Tradition and Islamic Orthodoxy: Philosophical and Theological Summae in Context." PhD diss., MLU Halle-Wittenberg, 2009.

El-Rouayheb, Khaled. *The Development of Arabic Logic (1200–1800).* Basel: Schwabe, 2019.

———. "Does a Proposition Have Three Parts or Four? A Debate in Later Arabic Logic." *Oriens* 44 (2016): 301–31.

———. "Impossible Antecedents and Their Consequences: Some Thirteenth-Century Arabic Discussions." *History and Philosophy of Logic* 30 (2009): 209–25.

———. "Al-Kātibī al-Qazwīnī." In *Encyclopaedia of Islam*, 3rd ed.

———. "Post-Avicennan Logicians on the Subject Matter of Logic: Some Thirteenth- and Fourteenth-Century Discussions." *Arabic Sciences and Philosophy* 22 (2012): 69–90.

———. *Relational Syllogisms and the History of Arabic Logic, 900–1900*. Islamic Philosophy, Theology and Science. Texts and Studies, vol. 80. Leiden, Netherlands: Brill, 2010.

———. "Sunni Muslim Scholars on the Status of Logic, 1500–1800." *Islamic Law and Society* 2 (2004): 213–32.

———. "*Takmīl al-Manṭiq*: A Sixteenth-Century Arabic Manual on Logic." In *Illuminationist Texts and Textual Studies: Essays in Memory of Hossein Ziai*, edited by Ahmed Alwishah, Ali Gheissari, and John Walbridge, 197–256. Leiden, Netherlands: Brill, 2018.

———. "Two Fourteenth-Century Islamic Philosophers: Ibn Mubārakshāh al-Bukhārī and Mullāzāde al-Kharziyānī." *Oriens* 48, 3–4 (2020): 345–66.

Fallahi, Asad. "Fārābī and Avicenna on Contraposition." *History and Philosophy of Logic* 40 (2019): 22-41.

Al-Fārābī, Abū Naṣr. *Kitāb al-Ḥurūf*. Edited by M. Mahdī. Beirut: Dār al-Mashriq, 1990.

———. *Sharḥ al-ʿIbārah*. *See* Zimmermann, *Al-Fārābī's Commentary and Short Treatise on Aristotle's De Interpretatione*.

Al-Ghazālī, Abū Ḥāmid. *Al-Mustaṣfā min ʿilm al-uṣūl*. Būlāq, Egypt: al-Maṭbaʿah al-Amīriyyah, 1324/1906.

Gutas, Dimitri. "Aspects of Literary Form and Genre in Arabic Logical Works." In *Glosses and Commentaries on Aristotelian Logical Texts: The Syriac, Arabic and Medieval Latin Traditions*, edited by Charles Burnett, 29–64. London: Warburg Institute, 1993.

Gutas, Dimitri. *Avicenna and the Aristotelian Tradition: Introduction to Reading Avicenna's Philosophical Works*. 2nd edition. Islamic Philosophy, Theology and Science. Texts and Studies, vol. 89. Leiden, Netherlands: Brill, 2014.

———. "The Empiricism of Avicenna." *Oriens* 40 (2012): 391–436.

Hermans, Erik. "A Persian Origin of the Arabic Aristotle? The Debate on the Circumstantial Evidence of the Manteq Revisited." *Journal of Persianate Studies* 11 (2018): 72–88.

Al-Ḥillī, al-Ḥasan ibn Yūsuf ibn al-Muṭahhar. *Al-Asrār al-khafiyyah fī l-ʿulūm al-ʿaqliyyah*. Qom, Iran: Markaz al-Abḥāth wa-l-Dirāsāt al-Islāmiyyah, Qism Iḥyāʾ al-Turāth al-Islāmī, 2000.

———. *Al-Qawāʿid al-jaliyyah fī sharḥ al-Risālah al-Shamsiyyah*. Edited by F. Ḥ. Tabrīziyān. Qom, Iran: Muʾassasat al-Nashr al-Islāmī, 1432 HŠ/2012.

Hodgson, Marshall G. S. *The Expansion of Islam in the Middle Periods*. Vol. 2 of *The Venture of Islam: Conscience and History in a World Civilization*. Chicago: University of Chicago Press, 2004.

Ibn Khaldun, Abu Zayd. *The Muqaddimah: An Introduction to History*. Translated by Franz Rosenthal. Vol. 3. London: Routledge, 1958.

Ibn Mubārakshāh. *Sharḥ al-Shamsiyyah*. MS 616, fols. ob–122a. Zeytinoğlu Halk Kütüphanesi, Kütahya, Turkey.

Joseph, Horace W. B. *An Introduction to Logic*. 2nd ed. Oxford: Clarendon Press, 1906.

Kalbarczyk, Alexander. *Predication and Ontology: Studies and Texts on Avicennian and Post-Avicennian Readings of Aristotle's Categories*. Scientia Graeco-Arabica, vol. 22. Berlin: De Gruyter, 2018.

Kalbarczyk, Nora. *Sprachphilosophie in der Islamischen Rechtstheorie*. Islamic Philosophy, Theology and Science. Texts and Studies, vol. 103. Leiden, Netherlands: Brill, 2019.

Al-Kāshī, Afḍal al-Dīn. *Al-Minhāj al-mubīn*. MS Browne D.19(10) ff. 13r–75v. Cambridge University Library. Persian text is published in M. Minuvi and Y. Mahdavi, *Muṣannafāt Afḍal al-Dīn Muḥammad Marqī Kāshānī* (Tehran: Chāpkhāne Duwlatiye Īrān, 1337 HŠ/1959, logic vol. 2, 477–582).

Al-Kātibī, Najm al-Dīn. *Al-Mufaṣṣal fī sharḥ al-Muḥaṣṣal*. Edited by ʿAbd al-Jabbār Abū Sanīnah. 2 vols. Jordan: al-Aṣlayn li-l-Dirāsāt wa-l-Nashr: Kalām al-Buḥūth wa-l-Iʿlām, 2018.

———. *Al-Risālah al-Shamsiyyah fī l-qawāʿid al-manṭiqiyyah*. Edited by M. Faḍlallāh. Casablanca: al-Markaz al-Thaqāfī, 1998.

———. *Sharḥ Kashf al-asrār*. Enver Şahin, "Kâtibî'nin Şerhu Keşfi'l-Esrâr Adlı Eserinin Tahkîki ve Değerlendirmesi (Critical Edition and Analysis of Kātibī's Sharh Kashf al-asrâr)," PhD diss., Recep Tayip Erdoğan Üniversitesi, Rize, Turkey, 2019.

Keynes, John Neville. *Studies and Exercises in Formal Logic: Including a Generalisation of Logical Processes in Their Application to Complex Inferences*. 4th ed. London: Macmillan, 1906.

Al-Khūnajī, Afḍal al-Dīn. *Kashf al-asrār ʿan ghawāmiḍ al-afkār*. Edited by K. El-Rouayheb. Tehran: Iranian Institute of Philosophy and the Institute of Islamic Studies, Free University of Berlin, 2010.

Kilwardby, Robert. *Notule libri priorum*. Edited and translated by Paul Thom and John Scott. Auctores Britannici medii aevi, 23–24. Oxford: Oxford University Press for the British Academy, 2015.

Klima, Gyula. *John Buridan, Summulae de Dialectica: An Annotated Translation, with a Philosophical Introduction*. New Haven, CT: Yale University Press, 2001.

Klinger, Dustin. "Language and Logic in the Graeco-Arabic Tradition: A History of Propositional Analysis from the Hellenic Commentators on Aristotle to Theories of the Proposition in Arabic Philosophy, 900–1350." PhD diss., Harvard University, Boston, 2021.

Lameer, Joep. *The Arabic Version of Ṭūsī's Nasirean Ethics*. Islamic Philosophy, Theology and Science. Texts and Studies, vol. 96. Leiden, Netherlands: Brill, 2015.

———. *Al-Fārābī and Aristotelian Syllogistics: Greek Theory and Islamic Practice*. Islamic Philosophy, Theology and Science. Texts and Studies, vol. 20. Leiden, Netherlands: Brill, 1994.

———. "Aristotelian Rhetoric and Poetics as Logical Arts in Medieval Islamic Philosophy." *Bibliotheca Orientalis* 50 nos. 5/6 (1993): 563–82.

———. *Conception and Belief in Ṣadr al-Dīn al-Shīrāzī: Introduction, Translation and Commentary*. Tehran: Iranian Institute of Philosophy, 2006.

Łukasiewicz, Jan. *Aristotle's Syllogistic from the Standpoint of Modern Formal Logic*. 2nd edition. Oxford: Oxford University Press, 1957.

Marmura, Michael E. "Avicenna's Chapter on Universals in the *Isagoge* of His *Shifā'*." In *Islam: Past Influence and Present Challenge*, edited by A. Welch and P. Cachia, 34–56. Edinburgh: Edinburgh University Press, 1979.

Michot, Yahya. *Ibn Sīnā: Lettre au Vizir Abū Sa'd. Editio Princeps*. Beirut: Dar al-Bouraq, 2000.

Palmer, E. H. *A Descriptive Catalogue of the Arabic, Persian, and Turkish Manuscripts in the Library of Trinity College, Cambridge, with an Appendix, Containing a Catalogue of the Hebrew and Samaritan Mss. in the Same Library*. Cambridge: Deighton, Bell, 1870.

Peter of Spain. *Summaries of Logic. See* Copenhaver et al., *Peter of Spain: Summaries of Logic*.

Philoponus. *On Aristotle Categories 1–5*. Translated by Riin Sirkel, Martin Tweedale, and John Harris. Ancient Commentators on Aristotle. London: Bloomsbury Academic, 2016.

Porphyry. *Introduction. See* Barnes, *Porphyry: Introduction*.

Pourjavady, Reza, and Sabine Schmidtke. *Critical Remarks by Najm al-Dīn al-Kātibī on the Kitāb al-Ma'ālim by Fakhr al-Dīn al-Rāzī, Together with the Commentaries by 'Izz al-Dawla Ibn Kammūna*. Series on Islamic Philosophy and Theology Texts and Studies, vol. 5. Tehran: Iranian Institute of Philosophy and Institute of Islamic Studies, Free University of Berlin, 2007.

Al-Rahim, Ahmed H. *The Creation of Philosophical Tradition: Biography and the Reception of Avicenna's Philosophy from the Eleventh to the Fourteenth Centuries A.D.* Diskurse der Arabistik, vol. 21. Wiesbaden, Germany: Harrassowitz Verlag, 2018.

Al-Rāzī, Fakhr al-Dīn. *Mafātīḥ al-ghayb al-mushtahar bi-l-Tafsīr al-kabīr*. Cairo: al-Maṭba'ah al-Bahiyyah al-Miṣriyyah, 1938.

———. *Manṭiq al-mulakhkhaṣ*. Edited by A. F. Qarāmalikī and A. Aṣgharīnizhād. Tehran: Dāneshgāh-e Ṣāde, 2002.

———. *Muḥaṣṣal afkār al-mutaqaddimīn wa-l-muta'akhkhirīn min al-ʿulamā' wa-l-ḥukamā' wa-l-mutakallimīn.* Cairo: al-Maṭbaʿah al-Ḥusayniyyah al-Miṣriyyah, 1905.

———. *Sharḥ al-Ishārāt.* Edited by ʿA. R. Najafzādeh. Tehran: Anjuman Āthār wa-Mafākhir Ferhangi, 2005.

Rescher, Nicholas. "Avicenna on the Logic of 'Conditional' Propositions." In *Studies in the History of Arabic Logic*, edited by Nicholas Rescher, 76–86. Pittsburgh, PA: University of Pittsburgh Press, 1963.

———. *Al-Fārābi's Short Commentary on Aristotle's Prior Analytics.* Pittsburgh, PA: University of Pittsburgh Press, 1963.

———. *Temporal Modalities in Arabic Logic.* Dordrecht, Netherlands: D. Reidel, 1967.

Rescher, Nicholas, and Arnold vander Nat. "The Theory of Modal Syllogistic in Medieval Arabic Philosophy." In *Studies in Modality*, edited by Nicholas Rescher, Ruth Manor, Arnold vander Nat, and Zane Parks, 17–56. Oxford: Blackwells, 1974.

Sabra, Abdelhamid I. "Avicenna on the Subject Matter of Logic." *The Journal of Philosophy* 77 (1980): 746–64.

———. Review of Rescher's *Al-Fārābī's Short Commentary on Aristotle's Prior Analytics* (Pittsburgh 1963). *Journal of the American Oriental Society* 85:2 (1965): 241–43.

Al-Samarqandī, Shams al-Dīn. *Qisṭās al-afkār fī l-manṭiq.* Edited with notes by Asadallah Fallāḥī. Tehran: Mu'assasat Pizhuhishi Ḥikmat wa-Falsafah Īrān, 1441 HŠ/2020.

Sayılı, Aydin. *The Observatory in Islam and Its Place in the General History of the Observatory.* Ankara: Turk Tarih Kurumu Basimevi, 1960.

Al-Shāfiʿī, Muḥammad ibn Idrīs. *The Epistle on Legal Theory.* Edited and translated by Joseph E. Lowry. Library of Arabic Literature. New York: New York University Press, 2013.

Schöck, Cornelia. "Name (*ism*), Derived Name (*mushtaqq*), and Description (*waṣf*) in Arabic Grammar, Muslim Dialectical Theology and Arabic Logic." In *The Unity of Science in the Arabic Tradition*, edited by Shahid Rahman, T. Street, and H. Tahiri, 329–60. Dordrecht, Netherlands: Springer, 2008.

Smith, R. *Aristotle: Prior Analytics.* Indianapolis, IN: Hackett, 1989.

Smyth, William. "Controversy in a Tradition of Commentary: The Academic Legacy of al-Sakkākī's *Miftāḥ al-ʿUlūm.*" *Journal of the American Oriental Society* 112:4 (1992): 589–97.

Street, Tony. "Afḍal al-Dīn al-Khūnajī (d. 1248) on the Conversion of Modal Propositions." *Oriens* 42 (2014): 454–513.

———. "Al-ʿAllāma al-Ḥillī (d. 1325) and the Early Reception of Kātibī's *Shamsīya*: Notes towards a Study of the Dynamics of Post-Avicennan Logical Commentary." *Oriens* 44 (2016): 267–300.

———. "Avicenna's Twenty Questions on Logic: Preliminary Notes for Further Work." *Documenti e Studi Sulla Tradizione Filosofica Medievale* 21 (2010): 97–111.

———. "Kātibī (d. 1277), Taḥtānī (d. 1365), and the *Shamsiyya*." In *The Oxford Handbook of Islamic Philosophy*, edited by Khaled El-Rouayheb and Sabine Schmidtke, 348–74. New York: Oxford University Press, 2016.

———. "An Outline of Avicenna's Syllogistic." *Archiv für Geschichte der Philosophie* 84 (2002): 129–60.

———. "The Reception of *Pointers* 1.6 in Thirteenth-Century Logic: On the Expression's Signification of Meaning." In *Philosophy and Language in the Islamic World*, edited by Nadja Germann and Mostafa Najafi, 101–28. Berlin: De Gruyter, 2020.

Strobino, Riccardo. "Avicenna on the Indemonstrability of Definition." *Documenti e Studi Sulla Tradizione Filosofica Medievale* 21 (2010): 113–63.

———. *Avicenna's Theory of Science: Logic, Metaphysics, Epistemology*. Berkeley Series in Postclassical Islamic Scholarship. Berkeley: University of California Press, 2021.

———. "Ibn Sina's Logic." In *The Stanford Encyclopedia of Philosophy*, edited by Edward N. Zalta. https://plato.stanford.edu/archives/fall2018/entries/ibn-sina-logic/.

———. "Per Se, Inseparability, Containment and Implication: Bridging the Gap between Avicenna's Theory of Demonstration and Logic of the Predicables." *Oriens* 44 (2016): 181–266.

———. "Time and Necessity in Avicenna's Theory of Demonstration." *Oriens*, 43 (2015): 338–67.

———. "What If That (Is) Why? Avicenna's Taxonomy of Scientific Inquiries." In *Aristotle and the Arabic Tradition*, edited by A. Alwishah and J. Hayes, 50–75. Cambridge: Cambridge University Press, 2015.

Tabrīzī, Abū l-Majd Muḥammad ibn Masʿūd. *Ark of Tabrīz (Safīna-Yi Tabrīz)*. Tehran: Markaz Nashr-e Dāneshgāhī, 1423 HŠ/2002.

Al-Taftāzānī, Saʿd al-Dīn. *Sharḥ al-Risālah al-Shamsiyyah*. Edited by Jādallāh Bassām Ṣāliḥ. Qom, Iran: Dār Zayn al-ʿĀbidīn, 2012.

Al-Tahānawī, Muḥammad ibn ʿAlī et al. *A Dictionary of the Technical Terms Used in the Sciences of the Musalmans*. Calcutta: W. N. Lees, 1862.

Al-Taḥtānī, Muḥammad ibn Muḥammad Quṭb al-Dīn al-Rāzī. *Taḥrīr al-qawāʿid al-manṭiqiyyah fī sharḥ al-Risālah al-Shamsiyyah*. Edited by M. Bīdārfar. Qom, Iran: Intishārāt Bīdār, 2011.

———. *Taḥrīr al-qawāʿid al-manṭiqīyyah fī sharḥ al-Risālah al-Shamsīyyah*. Cairo: Ḥalabī and Sons, 1948.

Thom, Paul. "Al-Fārābī on Indefinite and Privative Names." *Arabic Sciences and Philosophy* 18 (2008): 193–209.

———. "Avicenna's Mereology of the Predicables." In *Mereology in Medieval Logic and Metaphysics: Proceedings of the 21st European Symposium of Medieval Logic and Semantics*, edited by Farbizio Amerini, 55–74. Pisa, Italy: Scuola Normale Superiore, 2019.

———. "Logic and Metaphysics in Avicenna's Modal Syllogistic." In *The Unity of Science in the Arabic Tradition*, edited by Shahid Rahman, T. Street, and H. Tahiri, 361–76. Dordrecht, Netherlands: Springer, 2008.

———. *Medieval Modal Systems: Problems and Concepts*. Aldershot, UK: Ashgate, 2003.

———. *The Syllogism*. Munich: Philosophia, 1981.

Al-Ṭūsī, Naṣīr al-Dīn. *Ḥall mushkilāt al-ishārāt*. Edited by S. Dunyā. 2nd ed. Cairo: Dār al-Maʿārif, 1971.

———. *Taʿdīl al-miʿyār fī naqd Tanzīl al-afkār*. In *Collected Texts and Papers on Logic and Language*, edited by M. Mohaghegh and T. Izutsu. Tehran: Tehran University Press, 1971.

———. *Akhlāq-Nāṣirī. See* Lameer, *The Arabic Version of Ṭūsī's Nasirean Ethics*.

Young, Walter Edward. "Concomitance to Causation: Arguing *Dawarān* in the Proto-Ādāb al-Baḥth." In *Philosophy and Jurisprudence in the Islamic World*, edited by Peter Adamson, 205–82. Berlin: De Gruyter, 2019.

Zimmermann, F. W., trans. *Al-Fārābī's Commentary and Short Treatise on Aristotle's De Interpretatione*. London: Oxford University Press for the British Academy, 1981.

Further Reading

The Tradition of Greek Philosophy in Arabic

Gutas, Dimitri. *Greek Thought, Arabic Culture*. London: Routledge, 1998.

———. *Avicenna and the Aristotelian Tradition: Introduction to Reading Avicenna's Philosophical Works*. 2nd edition. Islamic Philosophy, Theology and Science. Texts and Studies, vol. 89. Leiden, Netherlands: Brill, 2014.

Peters, Francis E. *Aristotle and the Arabs: The Aristotelian Tradition in Islam*. New York: New York University Press, 1968.

Al-Rahim, Ahmed H. *The Creation of Philosophical Tradition: Biography and the Reception of Avicenna's Philosophy from the Eleventh to the Fourteenth Centuries A.D.* Diskurse der Arabistik, vol. 21. Wiesbaden, Germany: Harrassowitz Verlag, 2018.

Traditions of Learning

Berkey, Jonathan P. *The Transmission of Knowledge in Medieval Cairo: A Social History of Islamic Education*. Princeton Studies on the Near East. Princeton, NJ: Princeton University Press, 1992.

Brentjes, Sonia. "On the Location of the Ancient or 'Rational' Sciences in Muslim Educational Landscapes (AH 500–1100)." *Bulletin of the Royal Institute for Inter-Faith Studies* 4.1 (2002): 47–72.

Eichner, Heidrun. "The Post-Avicennian Philosophical Tradition and Islamic Orthodoxy: Philosophical and Theological Summae in Context." PhD diss., MLU Halle-Wittenberg, Germany, 2009.

Ibn Khaldun, Abū Zayd. *The Muqaddimah: An Introduction to History*. Translated by Franz Rosenthal. Vol. 3. London: Routledge, 1958.

Makdisi, George. *The Rise of Colleges: Institutions of Learning in Islam and the West*. Edinburgh: Edinburgh University Press, 1981.

Pfeiffer, Judith. "Confessional Ambiguity vs. Confessional Polarization: Politics and the Negotiation of Religious Boundaries in the Ilkhanate." In *Politics, Patronage and the*

Transmission of Knowledge in 13th–15th Century Tabriz, edited by Judith Pfeiffer, 129–68. Iran Studies, vol. 8. Leiden, Netherlands: Brill, 2013.

Texts from Post-Mongol Marāghah

Madelung, Wilferd. "Nasir al-Din Tusi's Ethics: Between Philosophy, Shi'ism and Sufism." In *Ethics in Islam*, edited by Richard Hovannisian, 85–101. Malibu, CA: Undena, 1983.

Morrison, Robert. "What Was the Purpose of Astronomy in Ījī's *Kitāb al-Mawāqif fī 'Ilm al-Kalām*?" In *Politics, Patronage and the Transmission of Knowledge in 13th–15th Century Tabriz*, edited by Judith Pfeiffer, 201–29. Iran Studies, vol. 8. Leiden, Netherlands: Brill, 2013.

Ragep, F. Jamil. *Naṣīr Al-Dīn al-Ṭūsī's Memoir on Astronomy (al-Tadhkira fī 'ilm al-hay'a)*. Vols. 1 and 2. Sources in the History of Mathematics and Physical Sciences, vol. 12. Berlin: Springer-Verlag, 1993.

Al-Ṭūsī, Naṣīr al-Dīn. *The Nasirean Ethics*. Translated by G. M. Wickens. Persian Heritage Series. London: Allen and Unwin, 1964.

Studies on Arabic Logic

Chatti, Saloua. *Arabic Logic from Al-Fārābī to Averroes: A Study of the Early Arabic Categorical, Modal, and Hypothetical Syllogistics*. Cham, Switzerland: Springer Basel AG, 2020.

El-Rouayheb, Khaled. *The Development of Arabic Logic (1200–1800)*. Basel: Schwabe, 2019.

Kalbarczyk, Alexander. *Predication and Ontology: Studies and Texts on Avicennian and Post-Avicennian Readings of Aristotle's Categories*. Scientia Graeco-Arabica, vol. 22. Berlin: De Gruyter, 2018.

Rescher, Nicholas. *Temporal Modalities in Arabic Logic*. Dordrecht, Netherlands: D. Reidel, 1967.

———. "The Theory of Modal Syllogistic in Medieval Arabic Philosophy." In *Studies in Modality*, edited by Nicholas Rescher and Ruth Manor Rescher, 17–56. Oxford: Blackwells, 1974.

Strobino, Riccardo. *Avicenna's Theory of Science: Logic, Metaphysics, Epistemology*. Berkeley Series in Postclassical Islamic Scholarship. Berkeley: University of California Press, 2021.

Thom, Paul. *Medieval Modal Systems: Problems and Concepts*. Ashgate Studies in Medieval Philosophy. Aldershot, UK: Ashgate, 2003.

Translations

Ahmed, Asad Q. *Avicenna's Deliverance: Logic*. Studies in Islamic Philosophy. Karachi: Oxford University Press, 2011.

Chatti, Saloua, and Wilfrid Hodges. *Al-Fārābī, Syllogism: An Abridgement of Aristotle's "Prior Analytics."* Ancient Commentators on Aristotle. New York: Bloomsbury Academic, 2020.

Di Vincenzo, Silvia. *Avicenna, "The Healing, Logic: Isagoge": A New Edition, English Translation and Commentary of the "Kitāb al-Madḫal" of Avicenna's "Kitāb al-Šifāʾ."* Scientia Graeco-Arabica, vol. 31. Berlin: De Gruyter, 2021.

Zimmermann, F. W. *Al-Farabi's Commentary and Short Treatise on Aristotle's "De Interpretatione."* Oxford: Oxford University Press for the British Academy, 1981.

Index

جامعة نيويورك أبوظبي

NYU ABU DHABI

About the NYUAD Research Institute

The Library of Arabic Literature is a research center affiliated with NYU Abu Dhabi and is supported by a grant from the NYU Abu Dhabi Research Institute.

The NYU Abu Dhabi Research Institute is a world-class center of cutting-edge and innovative research, scholarship, and cultural activity. It supports centers that address questions of global significance and local relevance and allows leading faculty members from across the disciplines to carry out creative scholarship and high-level research on a range of complex issues with depth, scale, and longevity that otherwise would not be possible.

From genomics and climate science to the humanities and Arabic literature, Research Institute centers make significant contributions to scholarship, scientific understanding, and artistic creativity. Centers strengthen cross-disciplinary engagement and innovation among the faculty, build critical mass in infrastructure and research talent at NYU Abu Dhabi, and have helped make the university a magnet for outstanding faculty, scholars, students, and international collaborations.

About the Typefaces

The Arabic body text is set in DecoType Naskh, designed by Thomas Milo and Mirjam Somers, based on an analysis of five centuries of Ottoman manuscript practice. The exceptionally legible result is the first and only typeface in a style that fully implements the principles of script grammar (*qawāʿid al-khaṭṭ*).

The Arabic footnote text is set in DecoType Emiri, drawn by Mirjam Somers, based on the metal typeface in the naskh style that was cut for the 1924 Cairo edition of the Qurʾan.

Both Arabic typefaces in this series are controlled by a dedicated font layout engine. ACE, the Arabic Calligraphic Engine, invented by Peter Somers, Thomas Milo, and Mirjam Somers of DecoType, first operational in 1985, pioneered the principle followed by later smart font layout technologies such as OpenType, which is used for all other typefaces in this series.

The Arabic text was set with WinSoft Tasmeem, a sophisticated user interface for DecoType ACE inside Adobe InDesign. Tasmeem was conceived and created by Thomas Milo (DecoType) and Pascal Rubini (WinSoft) in 2005.

The English text is set in Adobe Text, a new and versatile text typeface family designed by Robert Slimbach for Western (Latin, Greek, Cyrillic) typesetting. Its workhorse qualities make it perfect for a wide variety of applications, especially for longer passages of text where legibility and economy are important. Adobe Text bridges the gap between calligraphic Renaissance types of the 15th and 16th centuries and high-contrast Modern styles of the 18th century, taking many of its design cues from early post-Renaissance Baroque transitional types cut by designers such as Christoffel van Dijck, Nicolaus Kis, and William Caslon. While grounded in classical form, Adobe Text is also a statement of contemporary utilitarian design, well suited to a wide variety of print and on-screen applications.

Titles Published by the Library of Arabic Literature

For more details on individual titles, visit www.libraryofarabicliterature.org

Classical Arabic Literature: A Library of Arabic Literature Anthology
Selected and translated by Geert Jan van Gelder (2012)

A Treasury of Virtues: Sayings, Sermons, and Teachings of ʿAlī, by al-Qāḍī al-Quḍāʿī, with the **One Hundred Proverbs** attributed to al-Jāḥiẓ
Edited and translated by Tahera Qutbuddin (2013)

The Epistle on Legal Theory, by al-Shāfiʿī
Edited and translated by Joseph E. Lowry (2013)

Leg over Leg, by Aḥmad Fāris al-Shidyāq
Edited and translated by Humphrey Davies (4 volumes; 2013–14)

Virtues of the Imām Aḥmad ibn Ḥanbal, by Ibn al-Jawzī
Edited and translated by Michael Cooperson (2 volumes; 2013–15)

The Epistle of Forgiveness, by Abū l-ʿAlāʾ al-Maʿarrī
Edited and translated by Geert Jan van Gelder and Gregor Schoeler (2 volumes; 2013–14)

The Principles of Sufism, by ʿĀʾishah al-Bāʿūniyyah
Edited and translated by Th. Emil Homerin (2014)

The Expeditions: An Early Biography of Muḥammad, by Maʿmar ibn Rāshid
Edited and translated by Sean W. Anthony (2014)

Two Arabic Travel Books
Accounts of China and India, by Abū Zayd al-Sīrāfī
Edited and translated by Tim Mackintosh-Smith (2014)
Mission to the Volga, by Aḥmad ibn Faḍlān
Edited and translated by James Montgomery (2014)

Disagreements of the Jurists: A Manual of Islamic Legal Theory, by al-Qāḍī al-Nuʿmān
Edited and translated by Devin J. Stewart (2015)

Consorts of the Caliphs: Women and the Court of Baghdad, by Ibn al-Sāʿī
Edited by Shawkat M. Toorawa and translated by the Editors of the Library of Arabic Literature (2015)

What ʿĪsā ibn Hishām Told Us, by Muḥammad al-Muwayliḥī
Edited and translated by Roger Allen (2 volumes; 2015)

The Life and Times of Abū Tammām, by Abū Bakr Muḥammad ibn Yaḥyā al-Ṣūlī
Edited and translated by Beatrice Gruendler (2015)

The Sword of Ambition: Bureaucratic Rivalry in Medieval Egypt, by ʿUthmān ibn Ibrāhīm al-Nābulusī
Edited and translated by Luke Yarbrough (2016)

Brains Confounded by the Ode of Abū Shādūf Expounded, by Yūsuf al-Shirbīnī
Edited and translated by Humphrey Davies (2 volumes; 2016)

Light in the Heavens: Sayings of the Prophet Muḥammad, by al-Qāḍī al-Quḍāʿī
Edited and translated by Tahera Qutbuddin (2016)

Risible Rhymes, by Muḥammad ibn Maḥfūẓ al-Sanhūrī
Edited and translated by Humphrey Davies (2016)

A Hundred and One Nights
Edited and translated by Bruce Fudge (2016)

The Excellence of the Arabs, by Ibn Qutaybah
Edited by James E. Montgomery and Peter Webb
Translated by Sarah Bowen Savant and Peter Webb (2017)

Scents and Flavors: A Syrian Cookbook
Edited and translated by Charles Perry (2017)

Arabian Satire: Poetry from 18th-Century Najd, by Ḥmēdān al-Shwēʿir
Edited and translated by Marcel Kurpershoek (2017)

In Darfur: An Account of the Sultanate and Its People, by Muḥammad ibn ʿUmar al-Tūnisī
Edited and translated by Humphrey Davies **(2 volumes; 2018)**

War Songs, by ʿAntarah ibn Shaddād
Edited by James E. Montgomery
Translated by James E. Montgomery with Richard Sieburth **(2018)**

Arabian Romantic: Poems on Bedouin Life and Love, by ʿAbdallāh ibn Sbayyil
Edited and translated by Marcel Kurpershoek **(2018)**

Dīwān ʿAntarah ibn Shaddād: A Literary-Historical Study
By James E. Montgomery **(2018)**

Stories of Piety and Prayer: Deliverance Follows Adversity, by al-Muḥassin ibn ʿAlī al-Tanūkhī
Edited and translated by Julia Bray **(2019)**

The Philosopher Responds: An Intellectual Correspondence from the Tenth Century, by Abū Ḥayyān al-Tawḥīdī and Abū ʿAlī Miskawayh
Edited by Bilal Orfali and Maurice A. Pomerantz
Translated by Sophia Vasalou and James E. Montgomery **(2 volumes; 2019)**

Tajrīd sayf al-himmah li-stikhrāj mā fī dhimmat al-dhimmah: A Scholarly Edition of ʿUthmān ibn Ibrāhīm al-Nābulusī's Text
By Luke Yarbrough **(2020)**

The Discourses: Reflections on History, Sufism, Theology, and Literature—Volume One, by al-Ḥasan al-Yūsī
Edited and translated by Justin Stearns **(2020)**

Impostures, by al-Ḥarīrī
Translated by Michael Cooperson **(2020)**

Maqāmāt Abī Zayd al-Sarūjī, by al-Ḥarīrī
Edited by Michael Cooperson **(2020)**

The Yoga Sutras of Patañjali, by Abū Rayḥān al-Bīrūnī
Edited and translated by Mario Kozah **(2020)**

The Book of Charlatans, by Jamāl al-Dīn ʿAbd al-Raḥīm al-Jawbarī
Edited by Manuela Dengler
Translated by Humphrey Davies **(2020)**

A Physician on the Nile: A Description of Egypt and Journal of the Famine Years, by ʿAbd al-Laṭīf al-Baghdādī
Edited and translated by Tim Mackintosh-Smith **(2021)**

The Book of Travels, by Ḥannā Diyāb
Edited by Johannes Stephan
Translated by Elias Muhanna **(2 volumes; 2021)**

Kalīlah and Dimnah: Fables of Virtue and Vice, by Ibn al-Muqaffaʿ
Edited by Michael Fishbein
Translated by Michael Fishbein and James E. Montgomery **(2021)**

Love, Death, Fame: Poetry and Lore from the Emirati Oral Tradition, by al-Māyidī ibn Ẓāhir
Edited and translated by Marcel Kurpershoek **(2022)**

The Essence of Reality: A Defense of Philosophical Sufism, by ʿAyn al-Quḍāt
Edited and translated by Mohammed Rustom **(2022)**

The Requirements of the Sufi Path: A Defense of the Mystical Tradition, by Ibn Khaldūn
Edited and translated by Carolyn Baugh **(2022)**

The Doctors' Dinner Party, by Ibn Buṭlān
Edited and translated by Philip F. Kennedy and Jeremy Farrell **(2023)**

Fate the Hunter: Early Arabic Hunting Poems
Edited and translated by James E. Montgomery **(2023)**

The Book of Monasteries, by al-Shābushtī
Edited and translated by Hilary Kilpatrick **(2023)**

In Deadly Embrace: Arabic Hunting Poems, by Ibn al-Muʿtazz
Edited and translated by James E. Montgomery **(2023)**

The Divine Names: A Mystical Theology of the Names of God in the Qur'ān, by ʿAfīf al-Dīn al-Tilimsānī
Edited and translated by Yousef Casewit **(2023)**

The Rules of Logic, by Najm al-Dīn al-Kātibī
Edited and translated by Tony Street (2024)

Najm al-Dīn al-Kātibī's *al-Risālah al-Shamsiyyah*: An Edition and Translation with Commentary
By Tony Street (2024)

Bedouin Poets of the Nafūd Desert, by Khalaf Abū Zwayyid, ʿAdwān al-Hirbīd, and ʿAjlān ibn Rmāl
Edited and translated by Marcel Kurpershoek (2024)

English-only Paperbacks

Leg over Leg, by Aḥmad Fāris al-Shidyāq (2 volumes; 2015)
The Expeditions: An Early Biography of Muḥammad, by Maʿmar ibn Rāshid (2015)
The Epistle on Legal Theory: A Translation of al-Shāfiʿī's *Risālah*, by al-Shāfiʿī (2015)
The Epistle of Forgiveness, by Abū l-ʿAlāʾ al-Maʿarrī (2016)
The Principles of Sufism, by ʿĀʾishah al-Bāʿūniyyah (2016)
A Treasury of Virtues: Sayings, Sermons, and Teachings of ʿAlī, by al-Qāḍī al-Quḍāʿī, with the **One Hundred Proverbs** attributed to al-Jāḥiẓ (2016)
The Life of Ibn Ḥanbal, by Ibn al-Jawzī (2016)
Mission to the Volga, by Ibn Faḍlān (2017)
Accounts of China and India, by Abū Zayd al-Sīrāfī (2017)
A Hundred and One Nights (2017)
Consorts of the Caliphs: Women and the Court of Baghdad, by Ibn al-Sāʿī (2017)
Disagreements of the Jurists: A Manual of Islamic Legal Theory, by al-Qāḍī al-Nuʿmān (2017)
What ʿĪsā ibn Hishām Told Us, by Muḥammad al-Muwayliḥī (2018)
War Songs, by ʿAntarah ibn Shaddād (2018)
The Life and Times of Abū Tammām, by Abū Bakr Muḥammad ibn Yaḥyā al-Ṣūlī (2018)
The Sword of Ambition, by ʿUthmān ibn Ibrāhīm al-Nābulusī (2019)
Brains Confounded by the Ode of Abū Shādūf Expounded: Volume One, by Yūsuf al-Shirbīnī (2019)

Brains Confounded by the Ode of Abū Shādūf Expounded: Volume Two, by Yūsuf al-Shirbīnī and **Risible Rhymes**, by Muḥammad ibn Maḥfūẓ al-Sanhūrī (2019)

The Excellence of the Arabs, by Ibn Qutaybah (2019)

Light in the Heavens: Sayings of the Prophet Muḥammad, by al-Qāḍī al-Quḍāʿī (2019)

Scents and Flavors: A Syrian Cookbook (2020)

Arabian Satire: Poetry from 18th-Century Najd, by Ḥmēdān al-Shwēʿir (2020)

In Darfur: An Account of the Sultanate and Its People, by Muḥammad al-Tūnisī (2020)

Arabian Romantic: Poems on Bedouin Life and Love, by ʿAbdallāh ibn Sbayyil (2020)

The Philosopher Responds, by Abū Ḥayyān al-Tawḥīdī and Abū ʿAlī Miskawayh (2021)

Impostures, by al-Ḥarīrī (2021)

The Discourses: Reflections on History, Sufism, Theology, and Literature—Volume One, by al-Ḥasan al-Yūsī (2021)

The Book of Charlatans, by Jamāl al-Dīn ʿAbd al-Raḥīm al-Jawbarī (2022)

The Yoga Sutras of Patañjali, by Abū Rayḥān al-Bīrūnī (2022)

The Book of Travels, by Ḥannā Diyāb (2022)

A Physician on the Nile: A Description of Egypt and Journal of the Famine Years, by ʿAbd al-Laṭīf al-Baghdādī (2022)

Kalīlah and Dimnah: Fables of Virtue and Vice, by Ibn al-Muqaffaʿ (2023)

Love, Death, Fame: Poetry and Lore from the Emirati Oral Tradition, by al-Māyidī ibn Ẓāhir (2023)

The Essence of Reality: A Defense of Philosophical Sufism, by ʿAyn al-Quḍāt (2023)

The Doctors' Dinner Party, by Ibn Buṭlān (2024)

About the Editor–Translator

Tony Street is a Fellow of Clare Hall at the University of Cambridge. He works on medieval Islamic intellectual history, focusing on Arabic logical texts written in the thirteenth century. He has held visiting positions at Paris 7, Berkeley, Oxford, and the Israel Institute of Advanced Studies. He is currently translating a commentary on the logic of Avicenna's *Pointers and Reminders* by Najm al-Dīn al-Kātibī's colleague and rival, Naṣīr al-Dīn al-Ṭūsī.

Milton Keynes UK
Ingram Content Group UK Ltd.
UKHW030803090824
446629UK00003B/43/J

9 781479 880249